To my Cousin Sandy!

Another Survivor!

Susan

(Don't lose this book)

Chemo & Lunch

One Woman's Triumph Over Hereditary Breast Cancer

Susan Winn

FITHIAN PRESS SANTA BARBARA 1990

Printed in the United States of America

Design and typography by Jim Cook/Santa Barbara

Published by Fithian Press
Post Office Box 1525
Santa Barbara, California 93102

LIBRARY OF CONGRESS CATALOGING-IN-PUBLICATION DATA

Winn Susan, 1956–
Chemo and lunch / Susan Winn
p. c.m.
ISBN 0-931832-53-5: $8.95
1. Winn, Susan, 1956– —Health. 2. Breast—Cancer—Patients—United States—Biography. I. Title.
RC280.B8W475 1990
362.1'9699449'0092—dc20 90-2784
[B] CIP

To my mother, Elda Steffens Hare.

Mom, you passed me a bad gene, but you also
loved me and gave me the strength
and courage to thrive.
I miss you.

Acknowledgments

Love and thanks to my dearest Kevin, who has supported me with every challenge I have faced.

I would like to thank Dr. Kelly Pendergrass, Dr. James C. Waldorf, and Dr. Lon McCrosky for their excellence in medicine and for their commitment to my health.

A special note of gratitude to Dr. Henry Lynch and his team at Creighton University in Omaha, Nebraska, for their work in hereditary cancer research, and for listening.

Contents

Preface

MY NAME IS SUSAN and I'm a thirty-two-year-old mother of four young children, recently diagnosed with breast cancer. I want to share my story with you and the incredible things my family has experienced, and, most of all, how I survived the diagnosis.

I was going to wait until the year 1996 to write this book; in the final chapter I would have finished the one-hundredth Boston Marathon at age thirty-nine. However, I must share the story now because I'm afraid I won't be alive in the year 1996. I really don't think I will die of cancer. I'm afraid I'll be killed on one of the Kansas City interstates driving to my weekly chemotherapy treatments.

The people of Kansas City are generally wonderful, but behind the wheel of a vehicle I've observed them to be dumb and rude. I can only compare them to the Minneapolis drivers (where I lived the first thirty-one years of my life). Compared to Minneapolis drivers, they are dumb and rude! It's a practice they self-describe as "sleep driving."

1956–1988, In a Nutshell

On a hot August day in 1956, Barbara Kay Hare was born at Abbott Hospital in Minneapolis, Minnesota. The next time my father visited the hospital, my mother had changed my name to Susan Mary. Barbara, Mary, Kathy, or Jane—it really didn't matter what generic 1950s name I was given. All six of us children inherited my mother's brown eyes. What is not known is which ones inherited the cancer gene she carried. I know I did.

I was the fourth born, with two older sisters, an older brother, and two younger sisters. According to psychologists, I should have suffered from the "middle child syndrome," but Dad says I never had that problem. My Aunt Lucille tells the story of my first day of kindergarten. She had called our house and the place was in an uproar because Susie was starting school. My aunt did not understand why this event should cause such a stir since I was the fourth kindergartner my parents had "sent off" to school. For me, every event in my life has been a major one!

I grew up in the 1960s and 1970s in a family I would describe as "terribly middle-class." My father worked as a correctional officer and my mother was a homemaker who did day care to make ends meet. We always had food and clothes, but not a lot of extras. In grade school I would have given my right arm for a box of sixty-four Crayola Crayons. Money must have been an issue to me because I grew into a frugal adult. Some close family members have unfairly described me as "cheap."

My parents did manage to save money, and family vacations were important to them. We always stayed at Best Western motels that had a swimming pool. Dad tells me that on a trip to the Black Hills of South Dakota I asked, "Why do we have the crummiest car at this motel?" I perceived my grade school friend, Rose, as being rich. She lived in a comparable house in our neighborhood, but there were only two children in her family. Rose had her own bedroom with a TV while I shared a dormer with four sisters! She also had a real fur hat, her parents drove an LTD, and she often ate out at nice restaurants. In retrospect, they probably weren't any "better off" economically than my family—it just seemed that way. Rose didn't have a box of 64 Crayola Crayons either! The one thing Rose did have—that money couldn't buy—were large breasts. I think she already had breasts when I met her in the first grade! I was a late developer and envied Rose and her breasts. I still envy Rose's breasts—not because of the size anymore—but because they're disease-free.

I believe my upbringing was typical of being middle-class in the 1960s. My mother was a strict Catholic and a disciplinarian. We were raised in the Catholic faith by her. My father had no formal religion, but did acquire some Christian values somewhere which he impressed upon his children. Mom ran the household; Dad brought home the paycheck.

I went to grade school at St. Bridget's, down the street from my house. I thought the public school children were "oddballs" and I feared the nuns and my mother. It was not the period of promoting self-esteem. I remember when I started violin lessons in the third grade, overhearing my mother telling the music teacher (nun), "She has no talent, but I want her to learn to appreciate good music." The saddest thing I remember about my childhood is being told I was skinny, had a big nose, and straight hair. I don't remember being told I was pretty. Because of this, I always tell my own girls that they are pretty. On the positive side, I knew I was loved by my parents.

The one quality I have, and have had since childhood, is a sense of humor. I enjoy making people laugh and I believe that a sense of humor helps to buffer us from the tragedies of life. Some of the things that have happened to me and seemed terrible at the time, actually turned out to be some of the funniest stories later on. I've carried that sense of humor with me throughout my life and it has helped me get through the tough times.

My mother died of cancer when I was fourteen years old. This is one tragedy that a sense of humor did not help me to endure. My oldest sister and brother had left home and my father was left to raise the remaining four girls (Dolly was sixteen, Corinne eleven, and Pammy only seven years old). Being a man of his generation, Dad was not programmed for this role, although he did manage to pull it together and do a very fine job of raising four, high-strung, motherless daughters. Because of my mother's death I believe we experienced a much closer relationship with our father.

At the time of my mother's death, Dolly and my mother did not have a close relationship. Dolly was intelligent, but lacked inner motivation and this frustrated my mother. Because I was the ambitious one, my mother favored me. I think my father was perceptive to this problem and, consequently, favored Dolly in order to balance things out. When my mother died I felt alone.

When my mother knew she was dying she "groomed" me to take over her role as housekeeper, and when she died, that's exactly what I did. The house seemed to be full with the sounds of screaming among the sisters. While maintaining good grades in high school and leading an active teenage social life, I also planned the family's dinner meals, did the grocery shopping, cleaned our house, delegated jobs to my sisters, and even did some of the yard work. My father did not force this position on me; I took it on myself. Dolly had a part-time job and, therefore, was not expected to do much around the house. She also resented her younger sister telling her what to do! I remember once she did not change the sheets on her bed for six weeks, and then finally did only because I made an issue of it. Corinne and Pammy also had difficulty with me running the house and giving them chore lists. As my sisters got older they took on more responsibilities. We all survived growing up, but the fighting was plentiful. Years later I learned how my father survived the noise—he was hard-of-hearing and simply turned off his hearing aids.

My sister Dolly got married in 1978 and moved to Missouri with her husband. Shortly after their marriage, she and her husband became "Born Again Christians." This was a bit difficult for my family to accept, especially from Dolly. Initially, I found it rather irritating. How could this sister of mine (who never was the model of Christianity) suddenly be following the Word of God? We all "tolerated" the newly-reformed Dolly, but were thankful that she lived far enough from Minnesota so we wouldn't have to hear too much about it! It took many years before I was able to appreciate Dolly's faith.

When I was diagnosed with cancer, Dolly, along with her young children, drove two and one-half hours to my house. She came to help out and to share some healing scriptures from the Bible with me. I lay on the couch in the family room, recovering from surgery, and she read to me. A thought crossed my mind then, and I wanted to laugh out loud. Fifteen years ago I would have never believed that there would come a day when Dolly would be reading the Bible to me and I would actually be listening! The most important thing I learned from my sister is that people change, and that we must accept them for what they are today and not hold their pasts against them.

I attended Grace High School in Fridley, Minnesota, a coed Catholic school. My four years of high school were pretty much typical—both wonderful and awful. It was a constant struggle to find out who you were and then to "fit in." By the time I was a junior, partying and drinking were my major social outlets. In retrospect, I was "wild," but part of me wanted to be a "good" person. One of my teachers, Mr. Thompson, had more influence on me than he probably realized. He gave me what I needed at that difficult time in my life—attention. He listened to me and laughed at my jokes and was such a nice person that I often thought I'd like to grow up and be as nice as him someday.

When I graduated from high school in 1974 I had specific goals for my life. I wanted a college degree, I wanted to be a nurse, and I wanted to join the Peace Corps. I received a Bachelor of Science in Nursing from the University of Minnesota in March 1978. When I fell in love my plan for the Peace Corps went "down the tubes."

My first five quarters of college were depressing. I lived at home, worked part-time as a nursing assistant, went to classes, and studied. My social life was minimal and dates were few. Then, in the midst of 50,000 students, my path and Kevin's path crossed at the University of Minnesota.

It was December 1975, and my friend Nancy had talked me into going to a fraternity party with her. As I walked down the steps into the basement of the frat house, I spotted a handsome male by the beer keg with short black hair and wearing a yellow sweater. It was Kevin and attraction at first sight! The feeling must have been mutual because shortly thereafter I felt a tap on my shoulder; Kevin asked me to dance. "The Bump" was popular then and he was a really good dancer. Thirteen years later, Kevin still wears that same yellow sweater.

He is four years older than I am, but our backgrounds are very similar: we were both reared in the same socio-economic class, our houses were within a mile of each others', his mother was a nurse, and we were both from Catholic families. Kevin is the fourth-born of five children; I am the fourth-born of six. Also we both had ambition.

We "courted" throughout the remainder of our college days, graduating in the spring of 1978, and were married in September of that year. I was twenty-two years old and Kevin twenty-six. Like many others in our generation, we were impatient and wanted everything immediately. The country was in a recession then and during our senior year we had looked at small houses and wondered if we would ever be able to own one, especially since we were both living at home and neither one of us could afford to buy our own deodorant! We wanted good jobs, marriage, a house, and a baby and had no conception of what fabulous things the next ten years would bring.

After graduation I got a job as a registered nurse on a medical surgical floor at Abbott Hospital—the same hospital where my life began. Kevin was hired as a pharmaceutical sales representative for Marion Laboratories. Although Marion's headquarters are located in Kansas City, Kevin's sales territory was Minnesota. We moved into our first home in November 1978, and our first daughter was born in January 1980. We enjoyed all this so much that we repeated the process several more times! On March 29, 1983, exactly four-and-a-half years after our wedding, I delivered our third child. At the same time we signed the purchase agreement to build our fourth house! We were having so much fun, but in retrospect, I can't believe the stress we inflicted on ourselves.

The only stability in our first ten years of marriage was Kevin's employment with Marion Laboratories. Our home life was constantly changing and I had several different nursing jobs. I worked for one year at Abbott Hospital as an R.N. before I was hired by the University of Minnesota as a staff nurse in their Neonatal Intensive Care Unit. Looking back I believe our first-born was conceived the week I had off between the two jobs! Consequently, I worked in this unit for only nine months, but continued to work on a part-time basis after the birth of our children. To me it was important, economically and professionally, to continue working. Most importantly, it gave Kevin the opportunity to care for the children he helped produce. He enjoyed the added income and respected my part-time career. Life, however, would have been less complicated if I had stayed at home full-time.

Following my first maternity leave I was hired to work in the newborn nursery at Unity Medical Center where I worked for four years (minus two more maternity leaves). I was one of the "young" nurses in the nursery; several of the nurses had been there since the hospital opened, fifteen years prior, and they are still there. I worked the night shift and we talked a lot. I learned from those ladies and they shared wisdom with me that only experience teaches.

The most memorable lesson I learned was from Margaret. She

was old enough to be my mother and we were very different from each other. She was always very calm and liked things to carry on smoothly; I was a bit more high-strung and didn't really care for the norm. Once in a while I was able to get a rise out of Margaret that gave me a sense of accomplishment for the day. One such time was in the room adjacent to the nursery where the physicians performed circumcisions on male babies. The nurse's job was to clean up the area after the physician finished, which involved clearing the surgical utensils off the circumcision tray. Also on the tray was the piece of foreskin that had been excised. We would wrap up the paper lining of the tray, with the foreskin inside, and discard it all in the wastepaper basket. I must have been in a hurry one day, and as I was discarding the paper, the foreskin flew out and stuck to the wall of the circumcision room! I thought it was such a comical sight that I left it hanging right there on the wall with a note which read, "Who lost this?" Then I went to lunch, leaving Margaret behind. The foreskin wasn't there when I returned from lunch, but from what I heard, it *did* get a rise out of Margaret!

One day Margaret told me a story about herself. She said that in the spring of 1965 she was a young mother living in Fridley, Minnesota. A tornado had just ripped through the Minneapolis suburb, leaving her house standing in the midst of the chaos. When the storm subsided the police were going door-to-door, making sure there were no injuries and that people were okay. When they knocked at Margaret's door she answered with tears in her eyes and began telling the policeman about her little pine tree in the front yard that was destroyed when the tornado struck. The policeman gave her a look of utter disbelief and said, "Lady, half the houses on your block are missing!" This story was an excellent illustration to me of putting things in proper perspective.

In 1983 I left my job at Unity for a job in the heart of the city which was to be my last job before leaving Minneapolis. The position was as a staff nurse in the Transitional Nursery (TN) at Minneapolis Children's Medical Center which is actually located within Abbott-Northwestern Hospital.

I worked in TN for a little over four years, and by the time I left

I was considered one of the older, more experienced nurses. This job was very enjoyable and it was difficult to leave. I had no way of knowing that soon my TN friends would become my cancer support group.

Because of the "cancer cloud" that I feared hung over me, I had always felt that I would not have a long life span. This influenced how I lived, and the decisions that were made in our marriage. One such decision was to have my children before the age of thirty because I did not want to leave young children as my mother had done. Our fourth (and last) child was born just before my thirtieth birthday.

I've always had a flair for life and believe strongly in grasping opportunities whenever they present themselves. Perhaps I could have relaxed a bit more if I could have been guaranteed living to old age. I was always ready for a fun time and we were involved with a group of friends who liked to party hearty! The Halloween parties were the best. Two other favorites were a MASH party and the New Year's Eve Hot Tub party that Kevin and I hosted in our front yard when the temperature was thirty degrees and it was snowing! However, as our families grew, and we matured perhaps, the parties slowly diminished.

Our good friend, Gary, organized annual, adult camping trips to Monticello, Minnesota, the last weekend in September. We left the children with babysitters and camped out for two nights. It was not uncommon for the temperature to dip below freezing and we consumed a lot of alcohol and shared lots of laughter and fun.

During the September 1984 camping weekend, I carried my humor a bit too far. We had a large turnout that year—twelve couples perhaps, with our campers surrounding the campsite. The campfire was in the center of the campsite and everyone was huddled around the fire on that cold September night, singing and telling stories. Rick and I decided to streak so we both went to our campers and undressed. Rick's camper was on one side of the campsite and Kevin's and mine was on the opposite side. I didn't have enough courage to go out completely nude so I wore only a bar jacket; Rick wore only boots! On a cue from me, we ran out of our campers, twirled around, arm-in-arm by the campfire, and then ran back to our campers. The crowd went wild with shock and enjoyment.

In retrospect, I must admit that this was inappropriate behavior for a wife and mother. Kevin could have enjoyed the humor in the streaking more if one of the streakers had not been *his* wife. His only comment to me on the subject was, "If you value your marriage, you will never do that again," AND I NEVER WILL! Our friend, Carol, a comedian by nature, was part of the group. Carol can be very blunt at times and has had a lot of fun in life shocking people. I felt a great sense of accomplishment that "streaking weekend" because for a change I shocked Carol by pulling a stunt that she wouldn't even do. Of course, Carol and a few of the other women didn't have much to say to me for the remainder of that camping trip; the men were as friendly as ever!

I would describe our marriage as a good one, but not perfect. I am more liberal, nag a bit, am usually on time, and am a Democrat. Kevin is conservative, procrastinates, is usually late, and is a Republican. We've both run three marathons and my best time is better than his. Despite all, we have a good marriage.

The first ten years of our marriage were tremendous. Besides babies and houses, we had the opportunity to travel together. We vacationed in Colorado, Scottsdale, Las Vegas, Key Largo, Phoenix, and we even traveled to Kansas City for a few company meetings. In 1982 we took a seventeen-day trip to Europe and visited eight countries. The untypical aspect of this trip is that it was probably the most inappropriate point in our lives to travel. Our daughter was two, our son thirteen months, and I was pregnant with baby number three. What initiated the whole European trip idea was that Kevin's brother was stationed in Berlin with his family. Again, with the cancer "cloud" over me, I felt strongly that we had to grab each opportunity when it presented itself. Kevin and I still cherish that trip.

The two of us never liked being average and a hobby we started after marriage was marathon running. Both of us were athletic, but never envisioned a feat such as running on foot for 26.2 miles.

During my eighth month of pregnancy with our second child, I set a goal to run a marathon. Before that time I had never run more than three miles. We were competitive people and that helped; I'd run four miles and Kevin would run five, so the next time out I'd try for six. Eventually Kevin and I were in marathon shape. Originally, our first marathon was to be in Berlin in 1982 while we were in Europe; however, I was pregnant with our third child by that time so Kevin ran the marathon with his brother.

Finally I got my day. Six months after the birth of our third child I completed the 1983 Twin Cities Marathon! Kevin wasn't there for this event—he was busy that day and I don't think he thought I'd really finish, let alone finish in three hours and thirty minutes! My oldest sister, Bunny, drove me to the marathon and waited for me at the finish. She had more faith in me than I had in myself.

Running was in my blood and Kevin was very patient with me. I went on to run Duluth, Minnesota's Grandma's Marathon in 1984, and qualified for the Boston Marathon which was held April 15, 1985. Kevin, my father, Bunny, and her husband, Jon, accompanied me to Boston to watch me complete the race. A friend from high school and a college friend were also there as spectators. It was an awful experience; I developed diarrhea about five miles into the race and did not recover until the seventeenth mile. I finished the marathon in three hours and thirty-five minutes, which is quite amazing considering the time I spent looking for toilets, and more often, perched in the bushes!

The important thing is that I actually finished the Boston Marathon! I was then a twenty-eight-year-old mother of three preschool children and I felt a great sense of accomplishment. It taught me that I could set high goals for myself, and with hard work and determination, actually achieve them. It also boosted my self-esteem. I continued to run, but had no desire to run another marathon after the Boston experience.

Not to be outdone, it was Kevin's turn to run in a few marathons. He completed Grandma's Marathon in Duluth in June 1985 and the Twin Cities Marathon in October 1986. With small children it would have been too time-consuming for both of us to train for marathons at the same time. In October 1987, we both went to watch the Twin Cities Marathon because friends of ours were running. Kevin had a bad back and I had a classic case of "runner's knee" (another "Boston" complication). Nevertheless, we were both inspired to run another marathon, together!

Our goal was to run the Twin Cities Marathon on October 2, 1988 (three days following our tenth wedding anniversary). Because of our competitive natures I thought that perhaps we were setting ourselves up for marital suicide. The training and teasing began immediately. Kevin said, "Wouldn't it be nice if we crossed the finish line holding hands?" My reply was, "If you're there when I get there, fine, but I'm not waiting for you!" Then he said, "*You* wait for *me?*" And on and on it went. We didn't know at the time that we would no longer be residents of Minnesota in October 1988.

Where the Hell is the Spirit?

WHERE THE HELL is the Spirit? That had been my attitude for a long time because I never felt Spirit-filled. The Holy Spirit never spoke to *me;* I did not feel God's presence in my life. The few times I really believed in miracles were during the births of my children. But that was soon forgotten as they grew into two-year-olds! I tried to be spiritual, went to weekly mass, and attended Bible studies at various times in my life; I went through the motions, but never really felt it. I was always trying to make some sense out of the world, but couldn't. Often I thought I was too pragmatic to be spiritual. As I approached thirty I had more doubts about my faith in God than ever before; it became a constant spiritual struggle for me.

Kevin's oldest brother, Philip, and his wife, Anne, were very instrumental in causing Kevin and I to question our religion, faith, and spirituality. Philip and Anne were devoted, active Catholics when we were first married and for a short while they even belonged to the same church as we did. Perhaps it was a gradual process for them, but from our perspectives, one day Philip and Anne denounced the Catholic Church and joined the Living Word Church, becoming "born again" Christians. In my words they had "flipped"! This change caused more than a small wave within Kevin's family who were devout Catholics, his father being a deacon in their church. No one was very accepting of their newly found faith, or the way they tried to impress that faith on everybody.

Personally I was frustrated by all of it. I didn't want to write Philip and Anne off completely because maybe they were right. I wanted to feel what they felt, but I just couldn't buy it. I both envied and despised them and sometimes felt that their "born again" Christianity removed them from reality. My attitude about Anne was that she probably wouldn't have taken a shit unless the Spirit moved her!

I had faith in the Bible and believed the answers would be there, but I found it frustrating to read and hard to understand. It seemed too open to interpretation and I thought that people used it to justify their own beliefs. I didn't know who to believe or whose interpretation to follow and, ultimately, became what I considered a "doubting Thomas." A friend, Pat, who could identify with my feelings—wanting God to knock at my front door and give me specifics on how to live my life—described herself as a "semi-religious agnostic."

Kevin, on the other hand, never doubted the existence of God. Even though Philip and Anne caused him to re-evaluate his life, he very much wanted to continue practicing the Catholic religion which had been ingrained in him since childhood. Even though I was in conflict, I believed it necessary that our children be raised within a belief system; a structured religion was necessary to accomplish this. We continued to practice the Catholic religion and have raised our children in that faith.

The most disturbing thing for me was the spectrum between the rich and the poor. The Bible instructs us to feed and clothe the poor—but to what extent? Kevin and I were fairly generous in our giving, but never to the extent that it affected our standard of living. As we slowly climbed the economic ladder I began to feel guilty. I didn't think it was right that we had nice things when there were so many hungry people in the world. However, I was too materialistic to give too much away and this was a real conflict for me. And, when we moved to Kansas we built a beautiful home—nicer than I had ever dreamed possible.

As much as I liked my new home, I did not feel very good about it. The span between the rich and the poor appeared even more evident to me in Kansas City. This caused more conflict in me that I was unable to resolve. Instead of trying to justify it, it was simpler for me to move God further out of my mind and my life.

Chris, one of my ex-co-workers, was a "born again" Christian who found her new faith after her husband of several years cheated on her. I felt Chris was using this "born again" stuff as a crutch to get her through her ordeal, and I enjoyed challenging her. Chris and I had several discussions on the subject of faith. I would ask, "Chris, why does it take a tragedy to find God's presence in your life? I want to have the belief *without* a tragedy!" I knew there were people who had faith without tragedies, but it seemed to me that a lot of people found the Lord through crisis. Chris answered, "Sometimes it just takes a tragedy. Sometimes you just need to hit rock bottom before you recognize God in your life." Perhaps my life had been too smooth. Little did I know that in a few months I would experience tragedy in my life and God's presence would become known to me. I didn't want to be hypocritical, but I couldn't deny the things that happened to me.

When I was diagnosed with cancer I didn't suddenly begin praying, asking God to heal me. I was not convinced that He would heal on earth. In retrospect, I wish I would have prayed *before* the biopsy; I was skeptical of the power of prayer. As a teenager I watched my mother die—watched her lying in a bed, praying her holy cards and the rosary. She prayed for God to heal her. My mother wanted so very much to finish raising her young children. She fought, she prayed, she believed, and she died. I still do not understand why God took my mother. The night she was taken to the hospital for the last time, I watched her. The body was so thin, her hair was gone, her skin yellow, and her abdomen terribly distended, and she was moaning in pain. Before she was taken away I finally mustered enough courage to enter her bedroom and ask her what I could do for her. She answered, "Susie, pray that I die." She had stopped fighting and I couldn't bear to have her suffer any longer. I prayed. Three days later my mother died. Why had God answered this prayer and not the prayers to heal her? I felt God had let my mother down, but she prayed to the very end.

It became very apparent to me after my cancer diagnosis that other people possessed a strong faith in the power of prayer. I was amazed at the multitude of people who were praying for me to be healed. There were prayer chains for me in Minnesota, Kansas, and Florida. When friends called or wrote to me I was impressed with their belief in God and how freely and confidently they spoke of their faith. I began to think that there must be something to this faith/belief, and if there is a God, how could He ignore so many requests? The one feeling I immediately experienced through these faithful people from God was strength. Kevin and I both received an inner strength that I'm unable to explain which enabled us to accept and cope with our crisis better than I would have ever anticipated.

Anne called after my mastectomies and she and Philip wanted to drive down from Minnesota to visit with us. I welcomed them, but was still a bit skeptical. Feeling emotionally and spiritually weak, I felt vulnerable and feared that they would take this opportunity to brainwash me into their "born again" faith. Kevin was scheduled to work the first day after their arrival, and I was actually afraid to be alone with Anne and Philip. If ever the Spirit spoke to me it was the night before they arrived. I was lying in bed and in my thoughts I heard, "Listen and be open to what Anne and Philip have to offer you."

Within an hour of their arrival at our home, I knew that I had nothing to fear. My perspective of them was somehow different from before. They were so positive that I was healed, and I needed that. They possessed so much faith in God that it was inspirational. Anne and Philip shared stories and healing scriptures from the Bible and weren't "pushing" their faith; they were receptive to me when I voiced my spiritual doubts. They stayed for two days and we really enjoyed their company. It was the first time in years that I felt close to being on the same wave length as they. To be honest, I did not agree with everything they believed; I still had the continuing conflict of the rich and the poor. Philip believes that if you tithe and put your faith in the Lord, He will reward you with material things. I do not believe that our economic successes in life come from God. Surely there must be poor Christians! I still believe that overindulgence in material things is a sin when there is an abundance of homeless, hungry people in the world. Where the line is, I do not know.

Despite our differences, Anne and Philip were of benefit to me. When they left, instead of praying and asking God to heal me, I was able to pray and thank God for having healed me. It was important to me that Philip was supportive of the medical course I was taking. After they left, however, I began to question my Catholicism. Could I be a "born again" Catholic? Certainly I could be a Catholic Christian—I didn't believe everything the Catholics preached either! Could I extract what I liked from each side? Why do there have to be sides, anyway?

This inner conflict reminds me of The Mumps Story. I'm not sure what exactly it illustrates, but it's a funny story. Our fourth-born child was planned to be our last-born and, consequently, we wanted a permanent form of birth control. I felt that since I had given birth to four children, the least Kevin could do was to have a vasectomy. For his own personal reasons he didn't want to undergo this surgery; therefore, I had a tubal ligation. Even though I knew this form of birth control was not favorable in the eyes of the Catholic Church, I had no reservations about this decision.

Our baby, Maureen, developed the mumps at five months of age. This was rather unusual since the mumps vaccine is not given until fifteen months of age. After some discussion with the pediatrician, we realized Kevin never had the mumps and was too old to have received the mumps vaccine. Following this discovery, Kevin went to his own physician in order to have a mumps titer drawn to indicate if he had ever been exposed to the disease. The titer came back negative, showing that Kevin was susceptible to catching the mumps from our baby.

The night Kevin's physician called to tell us that Kevin was susceptible to the mumps, we were on our way out to a Communal Penance Service at our church. We figured he could get the mumps on, or about, Christmas Day! One of the complications, of an adult male with mumps is orchitis (inflammation of the testicles); a rare complication is infertility. Kevin found no humor in the threat of mumps or its complications, but I laughed silently.

A Communal Penance Service is one in which Catholics gather in a group to reflect, confess, and receive absolution for their sins. To help us remember our sins the priest delivered a sermon, stating each Commandment with elaboration on each one. By the time he got to the fourth Commandment I was feeling badly for having broken each of the four! I remember whispering to Kevin, "I'm batting four for four, so far." When the priest stated the fifth Commandment ("Thou shalt not kill") I felt somewhat relieved—I *knew* I had not broken that one. The priest then went on to question the congregation, "Have you ever had a vasectomy or a tubal ligation?" This was the first time I experienced guilt feelings about my tubal ligation. Whispering once again to Kevin, I asked, "Do you really think I'm a killer because I had a tubal?" His response was, "I don't know; that's between you and God." I remember feeling so irritated that he would separate himself from the situation that I shot back, "*You* deserve the mumps!" I guess that the middle of a church service was not the appropriate time or place to have continued that conversation, so we left the service early.

Kevin never did get the mumps, and I don't believe I broke the fifth Commandment. Despite conflicting feelings about the Catholic Church I will probably always call myself a Catholic. I don't believe that adhering to a particular denomination or religion will get you into, or keep you out of heaven. I believe that faith and how you live your daily life will determine this.

When I worked in the Transitional Nursery on the night shift, another nurse and I often had interesting discussions. Jeanette and I could solve most of the world's problems in a single eight-hour shift! I sometimes shared my family's cancer history, and Jeanette talked about her family's history of heart disease. She said she'd probably have a heart attack and be zapped off the face of the earth someday, without warning. I half-jokingly told her God knew He couldn't zap me; I "needed" cancer so that I would have time to repent! My joke soon became reality.

I knew a woman who was zapped a year ago in November 1987. Although I only met Carol once, I often thought about her tragic death. Like I, she was a nurse, and her daughter was in the same Brownie troop as my daughter. Her death happened only about a mile from our house. The roads were a little icy and Carol was involved in a fender-bender type accident. While she was outside her car discussing the accident with the other driver, an oncoming truck driver lost control of his vehicle, which slid on the ice and, consequently, hit and killed Carol. I had driven past the accident, but didn't find out until the next day who the victim was. It disturbed me that her husband and three young children had no preparation for her death. When I was initially diagnosed with cancer, I thought about Carol's family. I guess you can always find a situation worse than your own. I felt a little better off than Carol—at least I was given a warning. Yes, God knew that I couldn't be zapped.

The Cancer Tree

MY FIRST RECOLLECTION of cancer was at age nine when my maternal grandmother was diagnosed with the disease in 1965. It was such an awful disease that my mother could not even say the word. She cried at the dinner table and told us that Grandma was "sick." Back then people's perception of cancer was that it was a mutilating, deadly disease. I don't think people's perception has changed much nowadays. Certainly, what I witnessed over the years tilted my view so I held the same opinion of the disease. Despite the "cures" of cancer in modern medicine, "mutilating" and "deadly" are etched in my brain.

My grandmother fought the disease for two years while the family became "aware" of cancer. I believe she ended up with a colostomy when the cancer spread to her colon. At the same time, my mother told us that her cancer had begun in the "female organs" and that there had been a lot of cancer in the family.

When my grandmother died she was sixty-five years old; I was eleven. Since I was one of more than fifty grandchildren, Grandma and I were not emotionally close and I did not mourn her death. To a child, sixty-five is old, and the cancer aspect did not initially worry me. However, it soon began to worry me. On the Memorial

Day following Grandma's death we visited her grave and stopped at my maternal great-grandmother's grave. I was informed that she had also died of cancer. By the dates on her gravestone I calculated that she had only been forty-nine years old when she died. I remember experiencing a sinking feeling in my stomach when I realized that my mother was already forty years old. I was worried but little did I know that in four short years I would be staring at Mom's gravestone.

In February 1970, my mother had her gall bladder removed because of gallstones. Three months later she experienced an enlarged abdomen and underwent exploratory surgery which revealed massive metastatic cancer. By the time they diagnosed it, it was an open-and-shut case with no hope of survival. Her prognosis was two weeks to two months to live. With experimental chemotherapy and a strong determination to live, my mother survived for nine months.

The primary site of my mother's cancer was never determined, though it was thought to be gall bladder, in the biliary tree, or pancreatic.

My mother was from a large farming family, the third born of ten children (eight females and two males) and the first to die. Her death was especially difficult for my grandfather, who died in 1979 at age eighty-two, having endured the deaths of two more of his children and the diagnosis of cancer in another. My mother's death made me realize how devastating death can be, especially when it doesn't occur in the correct generation order.

The oldest, Uncle Joe, died in 1973 at age fifty. He lived in Washington and was the father of six children. I didn't know him, but the family story was that alcoholism killed him, not cancer.

The second child (and oldest daughter) was Aunt Anna Marie who also lived in Washington with her husband and two sons. I didn't know Anna Marie well either. She was a nurse, and as a child I remember thinking that she resembled my mother, although less attractive. Anna Marie died in 1974 of cancer at age forty-nine. Communication was limited and we were told she died of colon cancer. It wasn't until 1987 that my sister and I were able to determine that Anna Marie's primary cancer site was actually ovarian. This determination later became a very important discovery.

On the very same day the surgeons were operating on and diagnosing cancer in Anna Marie in Washington, surgeons were cutting into Aunt Mary in Arkansas who was diagnosed with breast cancer. I was a junior in high school when Dad told me the sad news of my two aunts. I remember the feelings of disbelief and fear—it was hitting closer to my heart. Although Aunt Mary lived in Arkansas, she'd lived in Minnesota for most of my life and we were friends. She was my Godmother and I was named Susan Mary after her. Mary was only thirty-eight years old at the time of her cancer diagnosis. She experienced a reoccurrence in the second breast at age forty-two, but battled the disease until her death on Thanksgiving Day, 1982 at the age of forty-six. Aunt Mary left a husband and an eight-year-old adopted son. I last saw Mary alive in August 1982 during a visit to Minnesota. She had lost most of her hair from chemotherapy and she reminded me so much of my mother that I was at a loss for words. Mary and her husband were on their way to Greece in a last ditch effort to save her. I don't know what the treatment was, but she was optimistic that she was going to find a medical cure in Greece. The next time Aunt Mary traveled to Minnesota, it was in a casket for her funeral and burial.

During the 1970s, a fourth daughter from my mother's family of eight girls was diagnosed with cancer. In 1976 Aunt Jeanne, the second youngest, was diagnosed with breast cancer at thirty-five years old. She lived in California with her husband and four young children. I visited her that year and I remember that familiar, hairless appearance. I was not particularly close to Jeanne and was apathetic enough at that point to believe that her days were numbered.

Aunt Jeanne taught me an important lesson—that cancer *is* curable. She's alive today, at forty-nine, fourteen years after her diagnosis. Jeanne has quickly become the person I want to model my life after. We have some similarities: our young age at diagnosis, the type of cancer and metastatic involvement, and similar cancer therapy. Also we both have three daughters and one son. Jeanne, however, had only one breast removed, followed by radiation and chemotherapy.

Jeanne always maintained that the Holy Spirit had some influence on her longevity—she doesn't associate her cure with medical treatment. Jeanne believes in the healing power of the numerous prayers prayed for her, and the strength she gained from praying herself. A few close relatives joked about Jeanne's analysis of her cure. I don't know how she was cured, but who am I to discount the power of prayer?

We were all relieved to see the 1970s end and wondered if the 1980s would be better. The 1970s had marked the deaths of my mother, maternal uncle, two maternal aunts, maternal grandfather, paternal grandmother, paternal aunt, and my great aunt. I guess I was too busy surviving the growth from adolescence to adulthood at the time to dwell on the losses. It wasn't until I looked back that I realized how dreadful those years really had been. I do not know that I hold a much more calloused view of death than my husband, who hasn't experienced many losses of people close to him.

By the 1980s it was apparent that no one single cure for cancer was going to emerge, and prevention became the focus. My maternal aunts, Corinne and Darlene, decided to take action rather than be "sitting ducks" and experience cancer like their older sisters. In 1981, at age forty-one and thirty-eight, respectively, they traveled from Texas to the Mayo Clinic in Rochester, Minnesota to undergo an experimental and controversial procedure called "breast stripping"—a prophylactic, simple mastectomy. The clinic had a limited knowledge of the familial cancer, but it was recommended by my aunts' physicians that "any female in the family should have this preventative procedure done at about age thirty."

I visited Aunt Corinne and Aunt Darlene in the hospital room they shared after their mastectomies. They both had new silicone breasts and about 200 stitches that they proudly showed me. With the surgery, they lost their breasts, but seemed to have gained some hope for the future. I decided then that when I turned thirty I would do the same. I was twenty-five years old and didn't know that age thirty would approach so fast!

My oldest sister, Bunny, was both smart and lucky. The oldest female grandchild, only five years younger than Aunt Darlene, she identified closely with the aunts and didn't want to be the first diagnosis of cancer in her generation of the family. In 1983, due to cystic disease and the fear of cancer, Bunny had prophylactic mastectomies at age thirty-six.

The early 1980s, cancer-wise, were thankfully uneventful. However, in 1986, my Aunt Kathryn was diagnosed with breast cancer. That made five of eight sisters having received the cancer diagnosis! Kathryn was just one year younger than my mother and they resembled each other, but Kathryn was more muscularly built, with hands larger than most men I know. She farmed along with her husband, and together they produced fourteen children. Most of the children were raised and had left the farm by the time Kathryn was diagnosed at age fifty-seven.

I'd always considered Aunt Kathryn an intelligent woman. I guess she'd become frustrated watching her sisters die hopelessly, and she developed a distaste for American medicine. I couldn't understand how this person who had had fourteen children (all single births), could fear a surgeon's knife. Perhaps it was simply mistrust. She refused surgical removal of her breast tumor and sought out her "cure" in Mexico. Calling it Hyper-oxygenation, they were apparently injecting hydrogen peroxide directly into her veins. She bought the story that this "cure" had been around for a century, but the American Medical Association and the FDA would not "welcome a breakthrough that could render 98 percent of all drugs, testing, and disease-related surgery obsolete." She believed that physicians didn't want to cure cancer, thus advancing their own personal financial status.

As relatives, we respected Kathryn's route of therapy, but most of us felt she was sadly wasting her money. I was frustrated because it was my opinion that as a post-menopausal female, her chances for survival with aggressive American treatment would have been great. Yes, she had watched a mother and three sisters die in the hands of modern medicine, but had she forgotten about Aunt Jeanne? Had she forgotten the cure? After several trips to Mexico, with minimal success, Kathryn made one last effort to save herself by a trip to Japan for another "miracle" treatment. She had spent the better part of two years consumed with saving herself from cancer, and in 1988 cancer was creeping throughout her body. She was thin, pale, and frail. The once muscular body was atrophied and Kathryn was dying in a Minneapolis hospital, under American medical care.

In July 1986, shortly after Kathryn's breast cancer diagnosis, our fourth child was born and I turned thirty the following month. I had accomplished my goal of bearing my children before age thirty, and it was time for me to seriously address the familial cancer and determine my course of action.

I remember my mother saying, "There's been a lot of cancer in the family," so my first step was to determine exactly *how much* existed. In the fall of 1986 I began a family tree that traced my ancestors and any incidences of cancer I could find. In the process I found more relatives than I ever knew existed. I also found a significant number of young cancer deaths, and that the cancer seemed to be a female disease. My maternal grandmother had five brothers, but was the only female child in the family. Because of this fact, I was interested in her female cousins and their children.

As a child I remember hearing about a university in Nebraska that was studying our family because of the number of cancer victims. The researcher was Dr. Henry Lynch of the Hereditary Cancer Institute in Omaha, Nebraska. I began corresponding with Dr. Lynch and found that he had not been kept up-to-date since the 1970s; he was only aware of the tip of the iceberg! I decided to complete my "tree" and send Dr. Lynch an update.

With the help of some long lost, distant relatives who had kept some excellent records, I was able to piece together a large tree dating back to the 1860s, when my great-great grandparents arrived in America from Prussia. Being Catholic, they were quite prolific! Joseph and Agnes Trunt produced fourteen children. My great-great grandmother, Agnes, died at age forty-four, pregnant with her fourteenth child. She died in a farming accident, but must have lived long enough to bear the child in her womb, Elizabeth, who also died. I can't imagine the hardship that family endured. Joseph, it is said, had two more wives after Agnes died.

Of the thirteen remaining Trunt children, seven went on to produce children of their own. The females from this family were of the most interest to me. Of these eight girls (including my great grandmother), two died young deaths; one from appendicitis and the other was killed. Five died from cancer, and only one lived to the old age of ninety-six. The cancer diagnoses had been made fifty to sixty years ago, with the limited diagnostic tools available in those days. I assumed the cancer hadn't been detected until it had spread elsewhere in their bodies.

By tracking the descendants of these seven producing children, the amount of cancer present became significant. Some branches were completely "clean," and yet other branches had multiple diagnoses. A year and a half into my research, my sister Bunny joined me in the genealogical tracing. We pieced together six generations and identified 650 descendants of Joseph and Agnes Trunt, confirming more than forty cases of cancer. The majority of the identifiable cancer was diagnosed as breast or ovarian cancer. Some of the others may also have been breast or ovarian cancers that spread to other parts of the body before diagnosis. Our biggest accomplishment was narrowing down the research to breast and ovarian cancer. We found that our grandmother's primary site of concern was ovarian, as was our Aunt Anna Marie's primary site. These specifics were very important to us in our research.

At this point I was convinced that there was a definite genetic link and that I should get myself an excellent physician who would take me seriously enough to put me on a surveillance program for early detection. I feared that cancer was heading my way. In February 1987 I received a call that my Aunt Corinne, forty-eight, had just been diagnosed with metastatic abdominal cancer. My heart sunk—more in fear for myself—because Corinne's diagnosis brought the number to six of eight of my mother's family with cancer.

Corinne had undergone prophylactic mastectomies and had had her ovaries removed as a preventative measure four years previously. Now her physicians were saying that she had metastatic ovarian cancer from ovaries that weren't even there—a rare occurrence. My initial reaction upon hearing Corinne's diagnosis was "Oh, shit!" I no longer *thought* I was at an increased risk for cancer, I felt I was *doomed.*

My correspondence with the Hereditary Cancer Institute of Creighton University was a cry for help. The institute was studying, and addressing, the hereditary link in cancer—a link with which I was becoming all too familiar with. In 1987 I sent Dr. Henry Lynch a semi-completed family tree, highlighting the cancer diagnoses. I also informed him about my Aunt Corinne's situation because her condition was very confusing to me. He must have been impressed because his nurse called me on the telephone and said that my family was indeed one that they would like to investigate in depth. I was elated to hear of their interest. *Finally* someone was saying yes, there is a problem in this family!

The "Practice" of Medicine and My Un-Diagnosis

MY ORIGINAL OB-GYN physician was a middle-aged man whom I believed to be competent and intelligent. My mother and oldest sister had gone to his group of physicians and so I started going to the same practice as a teenager. Dr. Bob Parker was round and balding, and his personality was one of a jolly and spirited man. He was wonderful to me during my ensuing pregnancies and always quoted cute, philosophical statements to me. During those pregnancies he'd reacted calmly to all my "major" concerns. I had enough confidence in Dr. Parker that if I would have ever experienced a medical emergency I felt he would have reacted competently.

Unfortunately, I liked Dr. Parker so much that I was blinded to his faults; I had mistaken his blasé attitude for calmness. In my early twenties, on several occasions, I had attempted to discuss the family cancer history with him. One of his most memorable responses was, "Well, you're lucky you don't have a family history of diabetes." I never felt that he shared my concerns; I suppose he wondered why a healthy, young woman would worry so much about cancer. On the other hand, he probably didn't give it much thought at all!

At age twenty-eight I discovered a small lump on the outer upper quadrant of my left breast. It was so small that I was embarrassed to schedule an appointment with Dr. Parker. However, I didn't want to ignore the lump either. I went to see a female internist that Kevin had recommended. She approached the situation in a serious manner and told me that I was acting wisely in having the lump checked out. I was sent for my first mammogram. The report was essentially "normal," indicating a small start of "cystic disease."

During my yearly OB-GYN examination with Dr. Parker I didn't tell him about the mammogram, but pointed out the spot/lump that I'd discovered. He did a breast exam and nonchalantly replied, "You have cystic disease which is more common than uncommon." Because of a disagreement with Dr. Parker regarding my inability to conceive another child, and because I no longer felt confident in his evaluation of my personal family history, a year later I sought a new OB-GYN physician.

My new OB-GYN physician, Dr. Tim Cohen, was a young, kind, sensitive man who had been referred to me by a mutual friend. He helped me, indirectly, with my infertility problem, and consequently I gained confidence in his medical knowledge. He followed me through my fourth pregnancy, but was on vacation when the birth occurred. He called me at home to see how I was doing after the birth and I was impressed with his concern.

In August 1987, I went in for my annual OB-GYN visit; I was thirty, soon to be thirty-one. I had decided that during this appointment I would discuss my familial cancer concerns with Dr. Cohen, and also to seriously discuss the prophylactic mastectomy idea. I knew that during the past year both his mother and sister had been diagnosed with breast cancer and thought that he would surely be a physician who would really listen to me. He listened, but I left his office feeling that he didn't feel that cancer was a real threat to me at my age. I requested a mammogram and he agreed with the request. He shared his mother's and sister's diagnoses with me and when I asked him if there had been a family history of breast cancer, he sadly said that he didn't know—his ancestors were killed in the Holocaust.

On the subject of prophylactic mastectomies, Dr. Cohen felt that the procedure was too experimental and cautioned me to research it better before making a decision for the surgery. He didn't tell me *not* to have the surgery, but I could tell that he didn't support the idea, either. It was then that I decided that the mammogram was a good diagnostic tool and also that I was too young to "chop" off my breasts unless I had developed problems. Unfortunately, if Dr. Cohen had supported the prophylactic mastectomies, I would have gone ahead with the surgery. Even though Kevin was pushing me to have the surgery, I felt he was too close to be really objective; I needed the push from a medical source.

Mammograms are not fun! After bearing four children I'd thought my privates had been insulted in every possible way but I was wrong! In my opinion, mammograms rank right above episiotomies. I had a second mammogram done in September 1987. The conversation went as follows: "Ma'am, can you move closer into the machine?" "Lady, this is all the breast tissue I own. Besides that, the corner of this machine is lodged in my ribs!" They tried to place my small breasts between two plates and then squished them flat! As I hugged that cold metal machine with my lead apron on, I wondered if males would routinely allow their testicles to be flattened in such a manner. It had to have been a male who invented this machine!

Dr. Cohen called me with the results a few days following the mammogram. He said that I had an area of small microcalcifications in the outer portion of the left breast. Microcalcifications? Just when I thought I knew all the terminology of breast disease, they threw me a curve. I'd never heard of microcalcifications in terms of breast tissue. Dr. Cohen assured me it was not a pre-malignant or malignant development; however, the radiologist recommended a follow-up mammogram in six months to make sure there were no changes. I hung up the phone and ran to my ten-year-old nursing school books to learn all about microcalcifications of the breast but the books yielded no such information.

Next, I requested the library in the hospital where I was employed to do a literary search for articles pertaining to microcalcifications of the breast. This search provided very little information. My sister then presented me with an article about the significance of mammographic calcifications in early breast cancer detection. The article stated that certain morphological characteristics, such as irregular shape, number, diameter, etc., were useful, but not conclusive in differentiating between cancer and a benign change in the breast. What I concluded from reading this article was that my microcalcifications were most likely benign. Because it was not cost-effective to biopsy all microcalcifications, some cancers could be missed. The article urged that all microcalcifications be biopsied to effect correct diagnoses. But, by the time I received this information, almost six months had passed and it was again time for the repeat mammogram. I dutifully made the appointment and had my breasts squished once again. I was more nervous during the several-day waiting period between the mammogram and getting the results than I had been before. When I called the doctor's office and requested the results, the receptionist was abrupt and said, "I remember seeing that report; it was normal and I filed it." I thought to myself, No, Lady, it couldn't possibly be normal because the first one wasn't. I should have chewed her out, but instead I kindly requested that Dr. Cohen call me to discuss the results. She called back within five minutes and said she'd found the report, it was in Dr. Cohen's box and he would be calling me. I think she realized her error.

Dr. Cohen did call me that day. He told me that the mammogram was unchanged and the radiologist recommended another mammogram in six months. I was on the verge of tears and remember having a difficult time talking with him for fear I would cry. I told him that my fifth aunt had just received a cancer diagnosis, we were soon going to be moving to Kansas, and I thought I should have a biopsy. His responses were, "But your mother didn't die of *breast* cancer. A biopsy is *so* invasive and the radiologists say that it doesn't warrant a biopsy. If you *want* me to refer you to a surgeon, I will." I said no, I felt perhaps I was overreacting after all, because I was a nurse, and had just enough knowledge to be scared but not necessarily enough to be rational or objective. I rationalized that the mammogram was a good diagnostic tool, the radiologist was a specialist at viewing these things, and everyone involved was aware that several of my aunts had breast cancer, etc. It was a real mental conflict for me. Just to be really sure, I decided to get a second opinion from an oncologist. I concluded at that point that OB-GYNs delivered babies and didn't view their job as including the diagnosis of cancer. I reasoned that an oncologist would look at the whole issue more seriously.

I was right. Dr. Jon Smith was just the man. With my family tree and previous mammogram films in hand, I went for my second opinion. Dr. Smith did view the family history with concern, and I felt pleased with his concern. He made me feel that I was reacting appropriately and that I had been wise to consult him. Dr. Smith examined me, looked at my tree, and viewed my mammogram films. He didn't think I had a malignancy, and said "pooey" to cost effectiveness when I told him of the article I'd read regarding microcalcifications. His advice: Yes, due to the family history my breast should be biopsied. He told me that unless one observed the tissue under a microscope they couldn't be sure of the pathology. He was so right! However, Dr. Smith went on to say that I need not "rush" to do this. He offered to refer me to a surgeon, but told me I could wait until I got settled in Kansas and have it done there.

During this appointment I also discussed the prophylactic mastectomies with him. His opinion was that it was not a matter of *if* I should do this, but *when*. He was right once more! Dr. Smith added that it would be a good idea for me to have the mastectomies sometime before age forty. I felt somewhat relieved that I would have a few more years to procrastinate in having this surgery. I also felt that I had a benign growth, and was confident in knowing it was a reasonable request to have it biopsied after getting settled in our new surroundings.

I don't remember when I first felt a change in my left breast.

Although I knew better, I hadn't examined my breasts each and every month. Yet, I did palpate them often, especially my left breast. After our fourth baby was born, and because of my decreased body fat (from running), I had shrunk to a size A-cup bra. Frankly, there wasn't a lot of breast tissue for me to feel but, despite the small size, a lot was "cooking" in there. I was aware of the small lump that initially had taken me to the female internist when I was twenty-eight, and that lump had not changed. However, there was an area on the outer aspect of my left breast that seemed to be thickening and just didn't feel like the rest of my soft breast tissue. This "thick" feeling had been there for several years and was the "cystic disease" Dr. Parker had referred to. Initially there wasn't a defined lump. I also mistakenly identified this as the area the microcalcifications were located. Later, I learned that the microcalcification area was located more axillary and that this was an entirely different change in my breast tissue.

If only I could have turned back the clock; a growth on your body is so subtle that it is difficult to detect change. I used to lie in bed at night and feel the area of the cystic disease over and over again, wondering if it had changed. But the mammogram indicated that it hadn't changed. Kevin used to watch me feel my breast and I know my self-examinations caused him to worry. I tried to reassure him (us) that it was the cystic disease and explained that the mammogram was such a fantastic piece of diagnostic equipment that it could even detect a "pinpoint" cancer. I told him, "Don't you worry, Kevin. I'm too young to have cancer." Still the examinations continued, with both of us feeling the cystic disease, followed by more reassurance that it couldn't be cancer.

I don't remember exactly when, but at some point around the time of my March 1987 mammogram, I began to feel a small lump in the middle of the cystic disease area. It felt like it was the size of a pea. The change had been subtle, but even Kevin could feel that pea. I realized it is "second guessing" on my part, but I should have demanded a biopsy in March and not cared if Dr. Cohen thought I was neurotic or not. If only I hadn't have put so much faith in that damn mammogram machine! If only I had had the prophylactic mastectomies at age thirty. If only. . . .

Sometimes the "cystic disease" would throb. It was more annoying than painful, but it did cause me to be concerned. I still harbored my plan of first getting settled in Kansas and then having this benign growth biopsied. I also planned to find an excellent oncologist who would take my families' history as seriously as I did. I knew that there had to be a physician who would put me on a surveillance program so that any cancer would be detected in its very early stages. I was going to be "on top" of this and not fall victim to the disease like so many of my relatives before me had done.

Kansas City, Here We Come!

I WILL BE HONEST—I did not want to move to Kansas! Kevin was a pharmaceutical salesman for Marion Laboratories, home-based in Kansas City, Missouri. I knew that if he had aspirations of doing something other than being a sales representative within Marion, we would eventually have to move. For nearly ten years he had been happy as a sales rep, and I was happy for him. Perhaps it was an early mid-life crisis, but Kevin decided he needed to move on to other areas within the company. Although I supported him, I secretly hoped it would never happen. After several interviews, Kevin was offered a position as a sales training associate in the home office. He was elated; I was sick in the pit of my stomach!

I felt sure all my happiness was over. Our life had been so stable—we'd made it almost five years in our home, a real record for us. I loved my job; economically we were secure; I liked my house; the children were assimilated in the school system and its surrounding activities. Why now? Why did I have to give up my security for his ambitions? We'd lived in Minnesota all our lives and our friends and relatives were all in Minnesota. "Kevin, are you sure this is what you want?" I was truly fearful of moving to Kansas and being totally miserable for the rest of my life!

On Easter Sunday, April 3, 1987, a rainy, dreary, depressing day, Kevin left Minnesota in his car to drive the eight hours it would take him to get to Kansas City and his new job. He was going to be living in an apartment for three months until the children and I could follow him; we wanted to wait until the children had finished that school year, and we were building house number five in Kansas. Those months of being apart gave me time to contemplate the whole matter of being a "displaced" person. Single motherhood wasn't nearly as bad as I had anticipated. I joked that this was a trial separation: maybe I would move to Kansas, and then again maybe I wouldn't—maybe I'd just send Kevin a letter requesting child support! Although most of those three months went smoothly, I remember the night the toilet ran over. I emotionally lost it and made Kathryn call her father in Kansas City to tell him her mother was crying while plunging the toilet. I didn't care that there wasn't anything Kevin could do to unplug the toilet long distance, but I wanted him to know about my frustration. I kept my sanity by hiring a babysitter so I could keep on running, continuing my marathon training in Minnesota while Kevin kept in training in Kansas City. He promised me we would return to Minnesota in October 1988, to run the Twin Cities Marathon as we had originally planned. We both mailed in our applications. His stated he was a Kansas resident; mine said I was a resident of Minnesota. I wasn't ready to let go.

On July 17, 1988, flight number 104 arrived at the Kansas City International Airport at 5:43 P.M. Kevin was at the gate to greet our four children, my oldest sister, Bunny, and me. It was not a particularly joyous reunion. I was sleep-deprived and had just spent one hour in an enclosed area with our offspring. In addition to that ordeal, the night before we left, our neighbor had come to our door asking me to return the sledge hammer that Kevin had borrowed six months previously. I had to tell him that his precious hammer was probably in the moving van on its way to Kansas. Kevin couldn't understand why I continued to dwell on the "hammer" situation when I had so many more important problems to face in this move. I couldn't tell him that the real source of my irritation was that I felt that my life had ended when our plane took off in Minneapolis. After a margarita and dinner at Chi Chi's I felt better and decided that since we had made the move, we should make the best of it, for the sake of the children! I thought, Who knows, maybe in a few years I will be able to say that Kansas *is* home. Maybe.

My description of my new life in Kansas is probably best illustrated in the letter I wrote to my former co-workers in the Transitional Nursery. Truthfully, I never thought I'd have much correspondence with those nurses after we moved, but they were to become my biggest support. Here is that letter:

> August 6, 1988
> Dear Friends in TN,
>
> Wanted to let you all know that things are hotter than hell in Kansas, and I arrived safely with my family. They don't tell the temperature here, they just say, "Hot and humid forever."
>
> No major adjustment problems, just numerous minor irritations, i.e., our mailbox is down the street, the McDonalds here won't take checks, reading the newspaper is meaningless, no Target [store], and no Old Dutch Potatoe Chips! The people I've encountered everywhere seem to be extremely friendly and kind. Even the girl who backed into my mini-van the day after we arrived, wrote me a nice note (with a check enclosed, of course).
>
> The move went rather smoothly. My sister flew down with us and stayed a few days. She was a lifesaver! She unpacked and I sort of walked around in circles. Maureen, (my babe), was upset by the move. She attached herself to my leg for the first week. Maureen also developed an ear infection after we arrived which made it all the worse. She's better now and has adjusted. The girls have found friends. Paul hasn't really found a good playmate yet. There aren't a lot of houses finished around us yet. I'm hoping as they fill, the boys will come.
>
> The house turned out quite nice. There is only one other

house done on the cul-de-sac and that is next door. The neighbors, Dr. (hunk) Bob and his wife, Chris, are very, very nice people. Chris is my age, they've been married the same amount of years, and have two girls the same ages as our two youngest. Everyone we've met so far in this neighborhood has TWO children. I'll be delighted when a large family of THREE moves in. Anyway, back to Dr. Bob, who's quite handsome, and built as well, and is an Emergency Room physician. If life gets too dull here, my plan is to collapse on his door step and check out his resuscitative skills! Truthfully, at this point, I'd rather have a smaller house, an uglier neighbor, and be back in Minnesota.

The people in this area are from all over: Nebraska, California, South Carolina, and Wisconsin. Haven't met a "true" Kansan yet, but that's okay. I think their accent is rather irritating. Then there's the man a few blocks over who mows his lawn with just shorts on, no shirt, and cowboy boots up to his knees. My guess is that he is from Texas.

No mice yet, but a lot of spiders in our new house! I opened my eyes one morning and Bridget was standing next to my bed dangling a dead daddy-long-legs in my face. Kathryn and Paul got a course in Basic Bathroom Cleaning 101. The thing about seven- and eight-year-olds is they think it's neat to have such responsibility and own their own toilet brush. Kevin declined my course, but promised he'd do a bathroom. I guess a brand new toilet brush didn't excite him.

My first debut into the Marion company social scene will be next week. As part of Kevin's job, he must escort a group of new associates to the home (mansion) of Mr. and Mrs. Kaufman for cocktails. Mr. Kaufman owns the company and is a multimillionaire. Can you see it? I think in order to maintain the "proper Marion spouse" image, I'd better keep my mouth closed and smile a lot. Kevin suggested perhaps I could refrain from slurping my wine through a straw.

Running in 101 degree weather has given the sport a whole new meaning. (YUK!) Kevin and I are still planning to come back for the marathon in October. I'm now attempting to train at 6 A.M. when the weather is cooler. It's amazing how cool 80 degrees can feel!

I'll be happy to hear from any of you. Any TN gossip? New pregnancies? Oh heck, just make something up about your favorite co-worker and send me a post card—life is dull in wheatland. I'll write again when I find work, although I haven't looked yet.

Take care.

Susan

The night out to the Kaufman mansion was quite an event; not the Kaufman's, but simply me getting there. The story is a lesson on vanity. It was Kevin's responsibility to pick up the group of new Marion sales associates at the Marriott Hotel. Their intention was to follow him in mini-vans to the Kaufman home where they were scheduled to arrive at 6:00 P.M. Kevin, wanting to be precise, went out the night before and timed exactly how long it took to drive from our home to the Marriott, and then to the mansion. He concluded that we had to leave our house at precisely 5:25 P.M. Naturally I wanted to look my best—not necessarily because we were going to the Kaufman's, but also because I was meeting several people from Kevin's new department for the first time. I always thought first impressions were important and that looks were a big part of that. Marion also seemed to be hiring a lot of young, attractive, female sales associates then, and I sure didn't want to appear like a housewife with four children. I was proud of my children, but I didn't want to look it!

I had an appointment for 3:00 P.M. to get my hair permed, cut, and styled. I had gotten a discount coupon from the Welcome Wagon lady and decided to try this unknown hairdresser. I was so concerned about my appearance that day; little did I know that in a few short months I would be facing losing not only my breasts, but also my hair.

Before I left the house for my hair appointment, Kevin said jokingly (as he always did when I got permanents), "Don't come home looking like Edna from the nursing home." I laughed along with him and drove off. CAN I HELP IT IF I PICKED THE SLOWEST HAIRDRESSER IN THE ENTIRE STATE OF KANSAS? At 4:50 P.M. I still had perm rollers in my hair and was beginning to feel panicky. In desperation I asked to use the telephone. I called Kevin and said, "Things are going a little slower than I anticipated. What is the latest we can leave?" Kevin yelled, "Get home *now!* We cannot be late!" I was visibly shaken when I told the hairdresser she had to get the rollers out right then because I had to leave. No time for styling! Well, my hair was so wet and so kinky that I was trying to dry it with Kleenex and fight traffic at an amazing speed as I headed home. I got home at 5:10 P.M. and have never changed clothes so quickly in my whole life. It was a nightmare. How could this have happened to an organized person? My hair was a disaster, with no time for reconstruction therapy. I wanted to cry, but didn't want to ruin my make-up besides. I did manage to take a minute to scream at Kevin for moving me to "this damn state," and off we went. Kevin, his nursing home friend "Edna," and the caravan of new Marion Laboratories sales associates arrived at the gate of the Kaufman mansion at precisely 5:59 P.M.! We were greeted at the door by Mr. Kaufman at precisely 6:00 P.M. I asked the bartender for a glass of wine and a straw! I tried to forget about my hair and actually managed to enjoy the evening, but then I didn't have to look at myself.

The remainder of August was pretty uneventful and I was thankful for that. It was beastly hot and humid, so I spent many days with the children at the community pool. The house was in good shape, and since money was getting tight I started thinking about getting a job as a nurse. Kevin kept pestering me to make an appointment with an oncologist he had met, but I wanted to wait until the children started school. I argued that my six-month mammogram wasn't due until September. Finally, wanting to get it over with and get Kevin off my back, on August 16th I saw Dr. Kelly Pendergrass.

The Diagnosis

I CAN'T SAY THAT my association with Dr. Pendergrass was a miracle, but I'm sure it was an act of fate. When Kevin was living in Kansas, alone those three months in the spring, Larry, who was Kevin's regional manager in sales, invited him over for dinner one evening. Kevin accepted the invitation and had dinner with Larry, his wife, and children. During the dinner conversation, Larry mentioned that his next door neighbor was an oncologist. Kevin's ears perked up and he told Larry that we were looking for an oncologist for when I arrived in Kansas. Larry happened to notice that his neighbor was in his backyard at that moment and suggested that he and Kevin go and talk with him.

Kevin talked with Dr. Pendergrass and gave him a brief history of my family. Dr. Pendergrass seemed to have knowledge of hereditary cancer and said he'd be glad to follow my case. Kevin called me that night, excited that he had found a doctor for me. I was glad that he had, but was somewhat skeptical of exactly who this physician was.

So, there I sat in Dr. Pendergrass's office waiting area, listening for my name to be called. I had enough time to second guess the whole appointment. "I'm thirty-one years old and in great shape.

What am I doing here?" "No, it's *my* life and someone had to look out for it." Oh, but will this doctor think I'm neurotic for seeing an oncologist when I don't even have cancer? I felt a little foolish, even with my mammogram films and extended family history in hand. But, I did have a small lump area and a few little things that felt like bee-bees; they were so small that Kevin couldn't even feel them. They must have developed over the past month. I also had the backing of Dr. Lynch and Creighton University for me to be on a surveillance program. I had also brought along some articles: "Surveillance and Management of Hereditary Breast Cancer," and "Surveillance and Management of Patients at High Genetic Risk of Ovarian Carcinoma"—just in case Dr. Pendergrass wasn't aware of the hereditary significance.

The first few minutes of the appointment I spent trying to justify my existence in his office. I said, "No physician in Minneapolis would treat me as high risk. I felt like I was being treated like the general population." The next few minutes I spent trying to decide if I even liked this guy and whether or not he appeared intelligent enough for me to trust him.

Dr. Kelly Pendergrass is short, handsome, with a well-groomed, mildly gray beard. He has wide, piercing eyes, and a quick, reassuring smile. He listened, and seemed to comprehend a nutshell version of my family history and my own personal health history. He talked very matter-of-factly about preventative options, such as prophylactic mastectomies and an oopherectomy (ovary removal), but I couldn't get an inkling of how much he really supported these options. He was simply presenting options. The first order of business, however, was the left breast.

Dr. Pendergrass examined me and viewed my old films and requested that I get another mammogram. His nurse was to call and schedule an appointment for me at the hospital. When she asked him what the diagnosis was, he told her "left breast mass." Left breast mass? That sounded awful! It sounded serious. Why couldn't he have told her that it was a follow-up mammogram or even a left breast lump? Mass! He also had some blood drawn from me that day for further detailed analysis.

Kevin and I returned to Dr. Kelly's office on September 2 for the results of the bloodwork and the mammogram. My blood work was perfect and the mammogram was essentially unchanged. Dr. Kelly really didn't believe it was a malignancy, but because of the family history and for our own peace of mind, he thought it should be biopsied and cautioned us not to wait too long before doing so. He also repeated what Dr. Jon Smith had told me in Minneapolis: "You really can't be sure unless it's looked at under a microscope."

By the time I saw Dr. Kelly, Kevin and I were already scared enough with the possibility of cancer that we had both made the decision that I should undergo the prophylactic mastectomies. We discussed this at length with Dr. Kelly and he seemed supportive of the idea. He suggested that instead of having a biopsy, I could have the prophylactic mastectomies and he would have the breast biopsied then. Why was all this happening at that particular time? We were planning to run the marathon, and I had just been hired for a new job that was to begin the week following the marathon. The children were starting a new school and it just didn't seem a good time for major surgery. With all that was happening in our lives we opted for the biopsy, and planned to have the mastectomies at a more convenient time within the next year. Kevin accused me of procrastinating with the mastectomies, but I still opted for the biopsy. My next appointment was to see Dr. Lon McCrosky, general surgeon.

Kevin did not accompany me to see Dr. McCrosky on September 14. I viewed this visit as a formality to meet the surgeon and listen to him describe exactly what the procedure would entail. The only question that Kevin wanted answered in that visit was "How soon after the biopsy can we get the results?"

My first impression of Dr. Lon was that he was tall, slender, and young—too young. I wanted a surgeon who had done this procedure more than once or twice! He looked younger than me! I remember thinking that I was entrusting my body to people I knew very little about. I do believe that these relationships are a matter of trust, and Dr. Lon had such a kind and gentle manner, he was very easy to trust.

Dr. McCrosky examined me and viewed my mammogram films. Then he talked and I listened. At this point the marathon was only two and a half weeks away and I didn't want the biopsy of this "benign" lesion to interfere with that. Dr. Lon did not talk like it was a benign lesion but explained all my options in case it turned out to be carcinoma. The options included a lumpectomy, a left mastectomy, a bilateral mastectomy (removal of both breasts), with or without breast implants and reconstruction. That familiar, sinking feeling in the pit of my stomach was back. Why was he telling me all this? The situation seemed so unreal, like "This can't be happening to me." Dr. Lon asked me if I wanted the biopsy then or did I want to wait until I returned from the marathon in Minnesota. I told him that "Before I came here today I was under the impression that I had a benign growth. You make it sound like I could have cancer." Although I liked him, I didn't like his answer. "Well, we really won't know for sure," he said, "until we take a look."

I knew that Kevin would be upset with my report of my visit with Dr. McCrosky and I was right. It was then that we decided to try to schedule the biopsy as soon as possible and hope that I would heal in time to run the marathon. Ten days seemed like a reasonable length of time for me to heal. Besides, if I didn't beat Kevin I would be able to use my sore breast as an excuse. The biopsy was scheduled as outpatient surgery, to take place on September 21, 1988. My in-laws had plans to visit us the following weekend and I asked Kevin to call them so they would be here the day of the biopsy. We really needed them to babysit the day of surgery, so Kevin could be with me at the hospital. When Kevin's mother arrived I told her that the biopsy would probably be benign, but just in case it wasn't, I was glad they could be there to support their son.

I know that we've all experienced moments in time that will forever be indelibly etched, in minute detail, in our memories. For instance, November 1963, when I was sitting in my second-grade classroom and the principal came into the room and said that President Kennedy had just been shot. Another one of those times was in June 1970, when I was told by my father that my mother had cancer. Then there was February 1987, when I was at work and I heard over the radio that the *Challenger* had exploded in flight. September 21, 1988 is one of those times. I was lying in the recovery room, awaking from the anesthesia, and Kevin was at one side of my bed, holding my hand, with tears in his eyes. Dr. Lon was on the side of the bed, touching my other hand, and speaking in a grave tone with a somber expression on his face. He said that the small growth he removed was "suspicious." The general atmosphere that surrounded my bed that day conveyed to me that "suspicious" meant "Susan, you'd better brace yourself for the results of the final pathology report." Shit! This is too awful to be happening to me. Kevin told me, months later, that he remembered the exact shirt, tie, and suit he wore that day. He also said he would never wear that combination again because it represents such a bad memory for him.

A few days later Dr. Lon called with the final report—*CANCER!* I was in disbelief: I was too young, I'd tried so hard to be on top of this thing and it had slipped right past me! I lost all objectivity regarding cancer and felt I had been dealt a death sentence. I guess I'd always thought that I would get cancer someday, but *not at age thirty-two!* Maybe God had punched my birthdate incorrectly into his computer. I thought, Give me forty-two, fifty-two, or even seventy-two (that would have fit into my life much better). I have small children to raise. This wasn't supposed to happen to me; I'm in excellent health, etc. I thought that running would protect me from this disease. I lamented that I had tried to make my doctors in Minneapolis realize that this disease was a threat to me. Boy, are they going to be surprised when they find out. Why me? and Why now? I was too depressed to be angry; my overriding emotion was *fear.* I was so scared; to me cancer meant death.

For two days following the biopsy results I experienced the deepest kind of depression and thought I would never be able to smile again. My beautiful children were a constant reminder that I would die and leave them motherless. My mother-in-law was with us to help hold the pieces together because I was unable to function. It was during this time that I began to witness a strength in Kevin that I hadn't known existed. This man that I thought would fall apart at such news, reacted in a totally opposite way. He was supportive and optimistic. He said: "You are not going to die. We are going to fight this thing and we are going to win!" I wanted so badly then to have possessed a deep spiritual faith to carry me through. In desperation I cried as I wrote to my TN co-workers. Here is an excerpt from the letter:

September 22, 1988
Dear Friends in TN,

I'm writing to you today because I desperately need your prayers and support. Remember, Lois, who had the expression, "to hell in a handbasket"? I never quite understood that, but I think my life just went "to hell in a handbasket." I have breast cancer and I am so scared.

Next week I will have a CAT scan and a bone scan. On Friday, September 30, I will have a bilateral mastectomy. I will then be followed with chemotherapy. My doctor is being aggressive and I am glad.

I'm so afraid I'm going to die and leave my babies. Kevin has been so kind and supportive, but this is so unfair to him. I'm angry because I wanted a biopsy last March and my doctor intimidated me out of one. I've never been a real spiritual person, but please pray that my lymph nodes are clean. Thank-you.

Susan

At that point I was experiencing a lot of ambivalence towards medicine. I also had some ambivalence towards myself for not being more assertive with my previous physicians. My former OB-GYN in Minneapolis, Dr. Cohen, called me after my surgery and I told him that I didn't blame him for my cancer, but felt that I had been intimidated out of having a biopsy. I also told him that I felt that he viewed me as a slightly neurotic woman when I had tried to discuss the family cancer background with him. He assured me that he didn't see me that way. He also assured me that he would view his patients having family histories of the disease, differently. I got some consolation from knowing that at least he had obviously lost some sleep over this diagnosis. I really was not experiencing anger towards him; I felt sorry for him. He was a good physician and he cared, but he was only human and, therefore, imperfect.

The mammogram is a machine, and it is also imperfect. After four separate mammograms, my actual cancer never showed! I had put too much faith in that damn machine. How is it able to pick up a pinpoint cancer and not detect something I could feel with my hand? Dr. Pendergrass told me that there's a 30 percent error rate with mammograms—15 percent will show a false positive and 15 percent will not reveal a cancer that's present. Why had I not heard that before? I was a nurse, trying to stay on top of it all. I should have never trusted my life to that machine!

I recalled Kevin urging for me to have the prophylactic mastectomies. The cancer scared him and the knowledge of my family tree only caused him to be more insistent. My comeback had often been, "How quick would you be to have your nuts stripped?" I had reacted negatively, wondering how I would explain to people that I had *elected* to have *non-diseased breasts* removed. For these reasons, I opted to have the biopsy first. I still feel that if I had received encouragement from a medical source I would have decided differently. Kevin says that I never listen to him and that was one time I should have listened to him. He was right, but I'm grateful he doesn't say "I told you so." That would hurt too much. I know that deep down, under all of his love, he is angry with me.

Experience has taught me that the practice of medicine is not an exact science, but it had never quite disturbed me as much as it did then. I was bothered that the decisions were mine: lumpectomy versus mastectomy, left side only or a bilateral mastectomy. Before that, I had made up my mind to have it all taken off because Aunt Mary had had only one breast removed and had had a reoccurrence in the other breast and died. I wanted to be as aggressive as possible and my new physicians supported that. But what if I had chosen a different option? I realize that it must be very difficult for a male physician to tell a female patient what should be done with her body, but why can't they say, "This is what I strongly recommend for someone in your position"? A friend of mine solves this problem by asking the doctor what he would recommend if it were his daughter in the situation.

Our next appointment before the surgery was with the plastic surgeon on September 26. He was blond, handsome, young, and had a smooth demeanor; he fit the mold of a plastic surgeon in my eyes. Kevin was with me and I was no longer depressed; I was in control, but still numb. Kevin asked numerous questions and I sat there while they discussed me as though I were an object. I told Dr. Jim Waldorf about my aunts who had prophylactic mastectomies in Rochester, Minnesota, in 1981. He said that he had been studying there at the time and possibly had even been in on their cases. This knowledge gave me false reassurance about this surgeon. When describing the reconstruction/implant procedure, Dr. Jim said, "I can't make them like God did." If I would have known him better, I would have replied, "I thought you surgeons were gods!" Instead, I bit my tongue. By the time we left Dr. Jim's office I was too tired to even form an opinion regarding my newest physician. As time went on, I found him very likable and I grew to respect his knowledge.

The plan was for the general surgeon, Dr. Lon, to remove the cancerous, left breast and lymph nodes. Then, Dr. Jim would step in and remove the non-diseased right breast, and insert implants on both sides. The question that almost jarred me out of control was, "Do you want to keep your right nipple?" Right nipple! Now I have to make a decision on my right nipple? "Can't I let you know the day of surgery?" Well, I decided to let them have it all, including the right nipple! Over the course of several months, the plan was for Dr. Jim to slowly inject solution into the implants to stretch the skin and muscle, and to attain the breast size that I desired. Once the skin and muscle had stretched properly, he planned to remove the implants and replace them with silicone bags. Following this procedure, he was to reconstruct nipples from tissue he would take off my abdomen and tattoo them brown. The whole thing was much more complicated than I had imagined, and I wondered if I would really have time for all of it. I asked why everything couldn't be done at one time (as my aunts and sister had done). The answer was that the cases were different; I had cancer, and advances had since been made in breast reconstruction.

The reconstruction was not so much for me, but for Kevin. There was so much for him to endure and I thought he deserved a wife that at least resembled a female. I was sure that he hadn't married me for my voluptuous body, but he's always enjoyed looking at women with large breasts. Here was my opportunity to have a really voluptuous body but all I really wanted to do was to live.

This Hospital is Not the Ritz

THE SURGERY for my bilateral mastectomies was scheduled for September 30, the day after our tenth wedding anniversary. It was a celebration of a wonderful past and an uncertain future, as we sipped champagne silently at home the night before. For the first time in our marriage we were afraid to look ahead. That was the day we'd planned to leave for our trip to Minnesota—our first trip back since leaving. We had planned to participate in the Twin Cities Marathon, but the day of the marathon I was in a hospital bed. In retrospect, running a marathon "together" may have been a good way to end a good marriage!

Following the surgery, I slowly regained physical and mental strength and my sense of humor began to surface again. In the previous ten years of my life I'd seen tragedy in so many other lives and wondered when "my bomb" would drop. My father-in-law used to say, "There's a bullet with everyone's name on it." The bullet had hit and I had decided to bite it; attitude was an essential part of recovery. The following letter best describes my surgical experience and the days that followed:

October 6, 1988

Dear Friends in TN,

Hi! The plant you sent was beautiful. The best part was getting a gift from you guys and not having to contribute to the kitty! The strength I receive from knowing you care is amazing. I appreciate those who have contacted me. Kevin thought that I should join some sort of support group, but I don't feel a need for that. How depressing to sit and listen to other sob stories. I told him I would write to you from time to time and pour my heart out.

You've probably heard bits and pieces. To be perfectly honest, IT'S THE PITS!! I had been taking aspirin four times a day for a knee problem while training for the marathon. That certainly got me in trouble! After several hours of surgery to remove my prized possessions, I had bled a lot. As I faded in and out of anesthesia, it was terrifying to hear them say my diastolic blood pressure was only 30. I survived only to suffer, (and I mean suffer, like worse than childbirth), because they would not give me any pain medication for the next four hours due to my low blood pressure. After a day and a half, my hemoglobin dropped to 6.0 and I had to consent to a blood transfusion. My surgeon tried to assure me that the risk of getting AIDS was minimal. I said, "Don't tell me about risk factors; I haven't done so well in that area."

Actually, I like my physicians. I have a general surgeon, a plastic surgeon, and an oncologist following me. They're all so young and handsome, it's unfortunate I can't enjoy this more. The plastic surgeon, over the course of the next several months, will make new breasts. Luckily, my breasts were really never one of my highlights. (Oh, really?)

Well, after four days of hospital stay, it was time to leave! When you look healthier than your care giver you know it's time. My roommate was an eighty-five-year-old comatose lady. A real ball of fire. Unfortunately, they sent me home with three Jackson Pratt drains, which get on my nerves. Tubes actually coming out of my body! I call them Jackson Pricks. I danced around the bedroom the first night home with my JP drains and asked Kevin if I was still sexually appealing. Poor Kevin will have to learn to lie better.

I had to take a break from this letter for an appointment with my plastic surgeon. He wouldn't take these damn tubes out. Do you believe I just traveled fifteen miles to his office to find out I looked good? I knew that!

Anyway, where was I? I'm home and feeling great. You've probably heard that three out of seventeen lymph nodes were positive for cancer. Just with mastectomies alone, they give me a fifty-fifty chance for survival. I had no choice on chemotherapy. Chemo will begin on October 18 and that will bring my survival to 80 percent. BIG GUNS TYPE STUFF—orally I will take Prednisone and Cytoxin. Weekly I will get IV Methotrexate, 5FU, and Vincristine. Seven to nine months of this stuff. Looks like I could lose my hair, but then again, that has never been one of my highlights either. I'm beginning to wonder what highlights I have.

This has been a battle both physically and mentally. For the first time in my life I have to fight depression. Basically, I'm okay. The trouble is I've always been a bit pessimistic and cynical. (Oh, really?) Everyone is so positive that I will be cured and I tend to dwell on the 20 percent. I hear all the cure stories and I think, Someone has to be in the 20 percent and die. I could die happy tomorrow, but I can't leave my children. It haunts me that I COULD DIE and leave my babies. I could deal with this all better mentally if they could guarantee my survival. I guess no one has a guarantee, so why should I? I think when I'm physically healed and able to start running again, I'll have a healthier outlook. Can't wait to jog with my new silicone implants. Wow!

Kevin has been a blessing. I worry about him though. He asked me how I wanted him to treat me. I replied, "Just continue to pamper the hell out of me." Would you believe he offered to give me his nipples? I told him I didn't want his nipples because they have black hairs! Do I really need nipples with black hairs?

It really has not been a totally bad experience, girls. I cannot begin to tell you of the outpouring of love my family has had the opportunity to experience because of this illness. If I could be spared my life, I could say it has been really positive. People have come from everywhere to help out. I've never known so many people have such a strong belief in God. Our lives will never be the same. People have been our source of strength and you in TN have helped. I love hearing from you. Keep the gossip coming. Bye,

Susan

We were desperately hoping the cancer was confined to the breast. Because the tumor removed at biopsy was only 1.2 cm, Dr. Lon speculated that the breast cancer would be Stage I, meaning it had not spread from the breast tissue. Wrong. After the mastectomies, he said there were some "suspicious" lymph nodes. There was that word "suspicious" again. By then I knew that Lon's definition of "suspicious" was cancer. I was feeling rather low the day the surgeon confirmed that the cancer had spread to the nodes and that we were at Stage II. Who knows where else in my body those microscopic cancer cells were waiting to attack. The final pathology report brought back that sinking feeling in the pit of my stomach.

On the last day of my hospital stay, the oncology clinician came to my room to explain the chemotherapy drugs I would be receiving and their side effects: nausea, vomiting, anorexia, diarrhea, constipation, skin rash, loss of hair, sores in the mouth, infection, numbness in my fingers and toes, bleeding in the urinary bladder, swelling, mood swings.... I envisioned the worse case scenario but this clinician assured me that I didn't necessarily have to get all of these side effects. Kevin was with me during her side effect presentation and I was feeling a lot of sadness. Before she could finish, there was a knock at the door; Mr. Onion appeared, dressed in tights! It was a singing telegram that Kevin had hired in an effort to cheer me up. I appreciated his efforts, but all the hats, balloons, and dancing in the world couldn't put a smile on my face that day.

For a period of time I became very egocentric. I didn't have the energy to look beyond myself and was receiving an enormous amount of attention. Too much had happened to me and I was overwhelmed. I could no longer read the newspaper or watch the news on TV. The presidential election was approaching and I had no interest in the results.

Following surgery, I had no desire to look at my chest the day they removed the large bandage. When I finally did take a peek, it wasn't as bad as I had anticipated. It wasn't a drastic change from my previously small breasts. The implants gave me a fullness so that I wasn't totally flat. When I arrived home and inspected my body in the full-length mirror, my attitude changed somewhat. Thinness no longer represented health to me; I viewed my body as skinny and diseased.

People were certainly our source of strength and I felt that God was reaching out to me through them. The house began to fill with flowers and plants as the news of my diagnosis seeped back to friends and relatives in Minnesota and throughout Kevin's company. I cherished each one because it showed me that they cared. The cards and letters came and I read them over and over. Friends had such faith in me, and I thought, Now why can't I have that much faith in God? Several referred to my battle with cancer as "the marathon of my life," and said they had no doubt that I would win. I was especially touched by friends from years past who wrote, and by acquaintances who took the time. I was pretty much hardened from tears by then, but occasionally a letter would choke me up. The following is one of those letters, written by the head nurse at Unity, one of my former places of employment:

> Sue,
>
> I've thought of you frequently since you left Unity and wish the very best for you. I heard about your difficulty with CA. I know you haven't been in your new home very long and I wanted you to know you have old friends who care about you

even though you are far away. You have been having some bad times with this I know, but I hope you will be able to continue your life to the fullest every day and not write yourself off for many, many years. You have a marvelous personality and a strong determination that will help you through these difficult times. There is not much I can do physically from so far away, but if there is anything I can do to give you any help and/or support, please feel free to ask. I would like to help if I can.

Carol

Each and every word of encouragement boosted my spirits.

October brought visitors from Minnesota. My oldest sister, Bunny, came to be "nanny" while I had surgery. Sister Dolly followed when I came home. My father came for a few days, and then it was Kevin's side of the family's turn. Anne and Philip drove down from Minnesota, followed by Kevin's older brother, Patrick, and his wife and two children. Soon after they left, Grandma Winn returned to help me recoup. We never felt alone and we weren't alone.

I became sensitive to what was said to me. If someone was overly optimistic, I wanted to say, "We're dealing with *cancer* here." If they were *too* sympathetic, I wanted to say, "Cancer doesn't mean death, we're talking *cure* here." For the most part, anything expressed was welcomed. I was cheerful and optimistic and my life seemed enriched.

There was, however, still that shred of doubt that would surface on occasion. Halloween was approaching and the children made paper cut-out skeletons at school, brought them home, and hung them up. Why couldn't they have made jack-o-lanterns? Skeletons were a reminder of my immortality and bothered me. Why wasn't I able to shake the doubt completely? I believed I was cured, but deep, deep down there was still some lingering doubt.

My next letter to TN was a bit more upbeat:

October 22, 1988
Dear friends in TN,

This was going to be a "short" note, but by now you know I'm a woman of many words. Have things calmed down in the nursery? Things have finally calmed down here. We've been bombarded with visits from our Minnesota relatives for three weeks straight. We love them all dearly and I know they all had a need to pay their respects and show their support, but enough! My mother-in-law left Friday; she's really great, but I sang the rest of the day. It is wonderful to be a "family" again and I can do whatever I want without someone saying, "You shouldn't be doing that yet."

I started chemotherapy last Tuesday. I had a flash of nausea when the nurse injected the drugs, but have been fine since. Luckily I only have to be on Prednisone for seven weeks. I told Kevin I could deal with losing my breasts and hair, but not a moon-shaped face! Prednisone can cause mood swings, so far the mood is up! The oncologist mentioned this week that chemotherapy will put me into menopause. (Oh, shit.) He went on to say that it really doesn't matter because when the chemo is over, the plan is to remove my uterus and ovaries. You see, I've finally proven to the medical world that I am an actual carrier of this "hypothetical" breast/ovarian gene.

Well, I'm about 90 percent recovered. Today I put on my red running tights (oh, what a sight), earphones, and went for a 5.4 mile run. The sky was blue, the sun was shining, and the trees were beautiful! "Pretty Woman" came on the radio and I was flying higher than a kite. Kevin was home washing windows. I told him I didn't have enough strength yet in my arms to do such work and he bought it.

Once you've had the big "C," every ache and pain brings back the doubt. You think, Am I kidding myself? But, for now I *have* to believe I'm healed. They'll have to prove me wrong. This whole experience has strengthened my belief in God; I've finally become more spiritual. However, today when I was running, these teenagers drove past me and made cat calls (must have been the tights). Without much thought, I flipped them the bird. It made me realize perhaps I haven't changed that much and reformation doesn't happen overnight.

I've met the nicest people through all this. My project now is to change my image from the "poor young mother with cancer," to the "healthy woman." I plan to start my new job November 7. Right now I feel like I can tackle just about anything.

Thanks for all the goodies—you guys are great! Take care.

Susan

I was given numerous books from people on self-help, spirituality, and mental attitude. I was diligently reading *Getting Well Again,* by O. Carl Simonton, M.D. In the book, Dr. Simonton describes the four psychological steps that occur in cancer surgery recovery. One of these steps is that with the diagnosis of a life-threatening illness, the threat gives the individual permission to act in ways that previously were not permissible. "Held-in anger and hostility can now be expressed; assertive behavior is now allowed." The only held-in anger of which I was aware was directed toward Dr. Bob Parker (my original OB-GYN) and the shabby way he treated me in September 1985. I didn't dwell on it, but every so often I would be reminded of the event and I would feel angry. I was mad at myself for not being more assertive with the old fart and always wanted to settle the score with him. Finally I did, in the form of a letter. The following letter is self-explanatory; it served the purpose of resolving my anger:

October 25, 1988
Dear Bob Parker,

I was thinking about you today and got this uncontrollable urge to write to you. Why? Because I was recently diagnosed with cancer. I really don't think I'm going to die; however, if that should be the outcome, you're the only person I have any anger towards right now and once I resolve that, I can rest peacefully. Also, so you know, I'm not angry because of the cancer. I'm angry because you treated me so rudely and unfairly.

I'm sure you don't remember me; let me refresh your memory a bit. My name is Susan and I was a patient of yours from the 1970s until September 1985. I had three beautiful children born in three and a half years and then you placed an IUD in me. After much discussion, my husband and I decided to complete our family with a fourth child (we were both fourth children). You removed the IUD and I couldn't get pregnant. I was pointing at the IUD as the "culprit," but never blamed *you* because I was knowledgeable to the risk of this device when placed. You never took my "infertility" seriously and stated, "It couldn't have been the IUD." You attributed it to "lack of lust" in a seven-year marriage. Your suggestion was to try for six more months and then a D&C.

Well, I had to get a second opinion on the D&C due to insurance. (You didn't believe this at the time either.) The other physician said it "could be blocked tubes from the IUD," and recommended a hysterosalphingraphy. Out of loyalty, I went back to you in September 1985 thinking you would be open to discussion. You became irritated when I was honest about the second opinion and said to me (which I'll never forget), "You are selfish and impatient!" I was choked to tears, didn't say a word, but fired you at that moment.

To finish the story, I went back to the other OB-GYN and he did the hysterosalphinogram. You were right! My tubes were clear. But he was Oh so right! He said sometimes just injecting the dye clears things up. Bob, I got pregnant seven days after that procedure!

I always wanted to tell you the end of that story and show you a picture of Maureen, a beautiful child (how selfish). I believe if I would have listened to you we would not have been blessed with her.

That's story number one. Have you had enough or do you want to read on? I'm feeling better. You see, we moved to

Kansas this summer and I don't have to see you at the hospital anymore, so I have nothing to lose.

On the subject of my breast cancer: I had a small lump when I was under your care but was too "embarrassed" to see you because I thought you would poo-poo it. I went to see a female internist and had a mammogram. It was a small spot of cystic disease. At my yearly exam, I showed you the lump and your response was, "You have cystic disease; that's more common than uncommon." I tried on a few occasions to express to you the strong family history of cancer. Your reply was, "You're lucky you don't have a history of diabetes." Well, Bob, how lucky am I? I'm thirty-two years old and that "common cystic disease" is now cancer. You should really be more in tune to disease, family histories, and what patients are saying. (I won't charge you for this advice.) I believe if I was still under your care I would be moving towards death. Your attitude was so blasé. It amazes me that you still practice "medicine" and they actually haven't yanked your license.

This letter may not be of any benefit to you, but I've wanted to get it off my chest (what's left of it) for a long time.

Susan

October was nearing the end and our lives had been in a constant state of upheaval for seven months. Kevin and I very much wanted to establish some normalcy in our family now that I was physically recovered and we had positive attitudes. I had begun chemotherapy with no adverse side effects. The children were adjusted in their new school and had made new friends. Things were going smoothly and we didn't need any more excitement, good or bad. Kevin had planned a business trip for the first week in November and asked me to go with him. I thought it would be good for us to get away—it was something we both needed. I was supposed to start my new job the week we returned from the trip to Puerto Rico.

On Friday, October 28, exactly four weeks following the mastectomies, I woke up at 5:00 A.M. in severe pain. The following letter to TN describes what transpired next:

> October 30, 1988
> Dear friends in TN,
>
> Hi! I need an ear from my TN support group. You guys are so fun to write to because you're nurses and can understand. Did you guess that writing is my therapy?
>
> I'm writing today because I'm back in the hospital and I am so depressed and bored. I'm feeling sorry for myself and knew that you would want to feel sorry for me too.
>
> I was four weeks post-op and things were going great. Then . . . ahh! Infection invaded my body! I woke up with the left "fake" breast and arm pain; then the big chill. Kevin brought me to the oncologist that morning sick as a dog.
>
> I have to stop here to tell you about lab technicians. In the last six weeks I've been stuck with so many needles that I've developed an aversion to them. I've been repaid for every innocent baby I've ever stuck! Anyway, I really don't trust these lab techs and sometimes by their comments, I *know* I shouldn't. For example, last week I told the lab tech that I don't like needles anymore. She said, "Neither do I; they talked me into this job!" The one I hear most often is: "I sure hope you have good veins." (Then you know you're in trouble.)
>
> Back to Friday. This lab technician at the oncologist's was supposed to draw a blood culture. There I sat with a tourniquet on my arm, and my tech said to the next tech, "How do you draw a blood culture?" Lab tech number two answered, "Here, 5cc's in each bottle and it has to be a sterile technique." Then my tech said to me, "Oh, my, they've changed things in the last twelve years." (My thoughts were, No, lady, it's *always* been sterile, and My God, I'm letting this person stick me!) I never realized how difficult it is to be Christian. (This gets even better.) Well, she actually hit my vein and was almost done when I said to her, calmly, "As soon as you get that needle out

of my arm, I'm going to lie on the floor and pass out." And I did just that.

When I came to, Dr. Pendergrass told me I belonged in the hospital. Can you picture this: Kevin (I think he's a saint by now) pushing me in a wheelchair, Maureen on my lap holding my blood culture bottles, and Bridget tagging alongside, through the corridor to the hospital. More needles, more drugs. (IV antibiotics.) Truly, girls, I long for a "normal" life; boring would even be nice.

It's Sunday and I had such wonderful plans for the weekend and I don't want to be here. (Sob, sob.) Kevin was to do some landscaping, Paul had a soccer game, and most of the weekend was to be devoted to Halloween fun. We wanted to bring the children to the Enchanted Castle, get costumes ready for school on Monday, and carve pumpkins. Tonight I was to pack for our trip to Puerto Rico. (Sob, sob.) Puerto Rico is out for me. I told Kevin if he could get a refund on my airline ticket, I would spend it on clothes and that would alleviate my depression some.

Girls, you know what is really scary for me now? I feel I no longer have *control* over my life's events. My life had always been so organized and planned. I'm so afraid to make plans.

Today was the Kansas City Marathon. The course went past the front of the hospital. As long as I was feeling so low, I went to the lounge to watch the runners go by to see how bad I could really feel. I wondered if I'll ever run another marathon. (Sob, sob.) To keep myself from crying, I began to visualize all those runners stamping my cancer cells to pieces as their feet hit the pavement. (This morphine is good stuff!)

Eleven-thirty A.M. Hey! Guess what? My oncologist just came in and he is going to drive me home. I get a four-hour pass to be with my children and do Halloween stuff! (The secret, girls, is bitching, complaining, and a few tears.) Now tell me, are there doctors like this in Minneapolis? You see, the big "C" has scared the little "c" (crap) out of me and that is what allows me to write letters such as this. I guess I've gained a lot of courage. Like I could say, "I have to get the heck out of this hospital." However, because I'm actually *not* going to die, I have to be careful not to abuse this new founded power.

The infectious disease doctor just came in; he feels the infection is around the implants and his recommendation is to continue antibiotics. But the implants must come out. (Oh shit.) My breasts were looking so good, too.

Well, gotta go—Dr. Pendergrass is waiting at the front of the hospital for me in his yellow Porsche. (Beats a yellow taxi cab!) I wonder if he'll bill me for this ride. . . .

Thank you for sharing my grief with me today.

Susan

There was another interesting thing that happened that Sunday. I was talking with Kevin by telephone, right before Dr. Pendergrass came to my room. We were both very depressed about the hospitalization and the uncertainty of the situation. After we ended the phone conversation, Kevin said he prayed and asked God to please let his wife come home. Within five minutes I called Kevin back and said, "I'm on my way home and I have a ride!"

The four-hour pass at home was great. First, I took a hot, sudsy bath. Then we carved pumpkins with the children and put together costumes for school the next day. I left instructions for the babysitter on how to do Bridget's outfit. Kevin and the children drove me back to the hospital in time for dinner and the next dose of IV antibiotics.

The next day was Monday, Halloween, and I anticipated a boring day in the hospital. Wrong. The morning started at 4:10 A.M. with the laboratory technician waking me to draw more blood. My room that day was a revolving door of nurses and doctors. By 2:30 P.M. my room was visited by my plastic surgeon, my oncologist, two IV clinicians, the infectious disease doctor and his two residents, my plastic surgeon—who returned with his nurse to inject Betadine solution into the implants—the two IV clinicians back again, more nurses, and a friend dressed in a clown outfit along with her two children. Everyone enjoys a little attention, but I had more than I needed and not the kind of attention I wanted. It was such an emotional day that I felt like I could laugh and cry simultaneously. When my friend appeared dressed as a clown, I cried.

There was a difference of medical opinions that day. The infectious disease doctor thought the implants needed to be removed in order to clear up the infection. My plastic surgeon, who had been off over the weekend, wanted to save the implants and treat with antibiotics. By that time I was feeling well and the signs of the infection were gone. The plan then was for me to go home on IV antibiotics for ten more days and hopefully prove the infectious disease doctor wrong. The plastic surgeon thought I would do well on oral antibiotics; however, since he had asked the infectious disease physician for his opinion, he felt he had better take his advice. I was feeling frustrated! I told the plastic surgeon that I was supposed to start a job in a week and if I didn't work, he didn't get paid!

Because I was to administer the IV antibiotics to myself at home, I needed what is called a PIC line (a peripherally inserted catheter). An IV line was put into a vein in my arm and threaded up to the atrium of my heart; it was to stay there indefinitely. Two IV clinicians came to my room to insert the PIC line; Linda and Kathy. These two nurses were really fun to relate to; they were the first nurses I'd had that were actually *older* than I. How I longed for a nurse to come in and say, "I've worked on this floor for fifteen years." I guessed they no longer existed, except in the nursery at Unity Hospital in Fridley, Minnesota!

Linda, Kathy, and I shared nurse stories while they did the procedure. We decided we should get together some night, drink some wine, and write a TV sitcom. The plot would center around nursing situations and it would be a hilarious hit, the amazing part being that all the stories would be *true*—no imagination would be needed. Kathy told me of a gynecologist in Kansas City named Dr. Hyman, and an orthopedic surgeon named Dr. Bone. I followed with the Minneapolis urologist by the name of Dr. Rivers, and about the time Dr. Parrot (a surgeon) had a "bird" because a nurse didn't have the supplies he wanted. Then there's the proctologist opthalmologist by the name of Dr. I.C. Bothends! We could have laughed and talked all day.

Then poor Kevin called and sounded so depressed. We both so desperately wanted *normal* back in our lives. My sister-in-law once told me, "But, Sue, you were *never* normal." Kevin had awakened at 5:00 A.M. and cried his eyes out. For the first time in our lives, instead of planning a bright future for our family, we were actually scared of what tomorrow would bring. I know the infection distorted our perception. Two years later we would be able to look back and say, "Wasn't that period in our lives awful? How did we do it?" We are convinced that the courage we now possess will make us better, stronger people.

On that Monday, Anne was the medication RN. She had hung the IV antibiotics for me, but was unfamiliar with the new antibiotic packaging. She hadn't activated the container correctly and all I received into my vein was normal saline solution. It was Linda, the IV clinician, who discovered the mistake. Anne was very embarrassed when she told me what had happened. I knew how she must have felt and told her not to waste time dwelling on it. Because she continued to brow beat herself, I told her my Gaviscon story to cheer her up. I also told her she could make it up to me by getting my bathroom cleaned! (I had missed the measuring pan the day before and pee'd on the floor. Also, there was some dried poop on my toilet that had been there since my admittance. I should have complained right away, but was too ill.) It bears reiterating that I was a patient in a hospital—not a gas station! This place was definitely not the Ritz.

The following is a good story about the station secretary: My IV line had come apart, and I put on the call light to get a nurse. The station secretary answered from the desk and I told her that I needed a nurse because my IV line had just fallen apart. The secretary's job is to relay this to the appropriate nurse (the nurses carried beepers for this purpose). Well, I waited and I waited, and I waited. Not wanting to insert the contaminated needle back into the line, I stood there holding the tubing. I had to shut off the IV pump so that the solution wouldn't run all over the floor. I was afraid that my line would clot off and there was still no nurse in sight. Then I put my light on again and when the station secretary answered again, I said, *"I need a nurse right now."* And, I waited and waited some more. I looked out my door for a nurse and there was none in sight. Finally, I held the door open with my foot, opened the drawer outside my room, grabbed a clean needle and alcohol wipe, and with one hand and my teeth, I *fixed the damn thing myself!* Of course, *then* my nurse made her appearance; she never got the message. It's not easy being a Christian!

Now for the Gaviscon story that I told nurse Anne: I had broken one of the basic rules that I had learned in nursing school—before administering any medication to a patient, you should know the purpose of the drug, the appropriate dosage, and be knowledgeable of the side effects. Unfortunately, when you're the only nurse responsible for distributing medications to twenty patients, that expertise is not always realistic and I wasn't one to scan the *PDR (Physician's Desk Reference)* during my only bathroom break of the evening. I was working the evening shift under the conditions just described—one nurse versus twenty patients needing medication. This was my first job as a nurse passing out medications on a medical-surgical unit. Mr. Peterson's doctor had ordered Gaviscon, an antacid. The two Gaviscon tablets were huge in size and were supposed to be chewed. Unaware that it was an antacid, I gave these two giant pills to an eighty-year-old man and made him *swallow them whole!* Someone must have caught on to my mistake the next day, because when I returned the next evening for the same assignment, someone had written in red ink on the medication card "Chew." So, with a smile on my face I went to give Mr. Peterson his evening dose of Gaviscon and told him that he could chew the tablets. He looked up at me and said, "Some nurse was making me swallow these whole and I think it was *you!*"

The ironic thing about this was that this incident occurred at the same time that Kevin had been hired by Marion Laboratories; the company manufactures Gaviscon and it was one of the medications Kevin was supposed to sell!

This reminds me of another nursing error I made (at least one that I will admit to) that is embarrassing, even ten years later. It was directly related to the fact that math was one of my favorite subjects and I had even taken calculus as an elective course in college. Somehow, though, I managed to proceed through grade school, high school, and college with the inability to read a number over 999,999!

Back to 1978 again—I was the charge nurse on the evening shift of the medical-surgical unit. A physician had written an order to administer 2,000,000 units of Penicillin IV every six hours to his patient. It was a new patient and I soon discovered that she didn't have an IV yet and that I would need to call her physician on the telephone to obtain an IV solution order. When I called, he had already gone for the day and I was connected to his partner who was on-call. This doctor was a real turd, but under the circumstances, I really couldn't blame him. The question that did me in was when he asked, "How much Penicillin did Dr. Smith order for this patient?" I looked at that number (2,000,000), and looked at the number, and pondered the question. It looked like two million to me, but gosh that seemed like so much, and I had never given Penicillin before. I couldn't say two million because I wasn't sure and accuracy counts! Finally, I mumbled, "Dr. Smith ordered two comma, zero zero zero comma, zero zero zero units of Penicillin." At least I was accurate! I can't remember his response, but I do remember that it wasn't pleasant. What is amazing is that they allowed me to continue being the charge nurse on that evening shift.

Back to Halloween Day in the hospital. All I could think about was missing trick-or-treating with the children. I wondered how Kevin was managing with all four of the kids and their excitement. I was so sad and wanted someone to sympathize with me, so I called my sister Corinne in Minnesota. Corinne had two young boys and I knew she would understand. I burst into tears as soon as she answered the telephone. We both cried for awhile, then talked, and by the end of our forty-five-minute conversation, we were both laughing. It was interesting to me that Corinne had dressed up her four-month-old. I had always dressed up my babies for Halloween, no matter what age they were. We had laughed at how silly this practice was. It had been a therapeutic conversation and I wondered what I would have done without sisters. I was still feeling emotional after talking to Corinne, so I began writing that night and the following is what I wrote:

Monday, October 31, 1988 9:00 P.M.

My "plan" tonight was to relax and go to sleep. So much for plans. I'm so hyped-up that I will use this energy to write some more. I've had so many drugs put into my body over the last few weeks that it is not surprising that I feel so strange. I was never the purist type, but now long to have my body rid of all drugs. The following is a list of drugs I've had over the past week:

1. Vitamins and Iron
2. Tylenol #3 (with Codeine)
3. Cytoxin (anti-cancer)
4. Prednisone (anti-cancer)
5. Methotrexate (anti-cancer)
6. Vincristine (anti-cancer)
7. 5FU (anti-cancer)
8. Primaxin (antibiotic)
9. Vancomyicin (antibiotic)
10. Benadryl (an antihistamine for an allergic reaction to Vancomyicin)
11. Morphine (a narcotic for pain)
12. Carafate (to protect my stomach from Prednisone)
13. Cirpo (antibiotic)
14. Redalin (a sleeping pill)

It's amazing what the human body can endure. My only consolation is that Kevin makes his living off the sale of drugs!

I talked with Kevin and the children tonight on the telephone after they got finished with trick-or-treating. It was almost as bad as missing Christmas. The kids were so excited. (Sob, sob.) Maureen was a pumpkin, Bridget was a witch, Paul a pirate, and Kathryn, a jellybean machine. It is hard for me to write this part because I'm crying and feeling sorry for myself. They wore the costumes to school today and Bridget won first place in her Kindergarten class! Being the competitive person that I am, I was disappointed that they all didn't get first prize. I guess I shouldn't have expected Paul to win; his was a store bought outfit. I missed Halloween with my children and I feel so sad.

I feel a little "funny" physically right now. It's real subtle, but I will try to describe it: right hand is warm and very slightly swollen. I feel slightly trembly and I have this after-taste in my throat. Occasionally I can feel my heart pound. Could it be the antibiotics? The Pic line? The RN in charge of this eighteen-bed unit came in and asked if she could do anything for me. I started to tell her about some of these symptoms I was feeling. I compared my right with my left hand so she could see the swelling. She could NOT see the difference and I knew she thought I was crazy. I was SCARED and wanted someone to know. It just wasn't worth mentioning any more symptoms. She attributed it all to my "stressful" day and then asked if there was anything she could do for me other than tell me that I'm okay. It made me so angry and that is one emotion that I haven't felt yet today. I don't feel okay! I'm writing now because I am angry and scared.

What I really wanted to write about tonight is my belief that there REALLY is a God. There have been just too many incidences that have occurred to leave the doubt that I have been burdened with for so long. I believe they were acts of God. There have been so many coincidences in our life lately. This morning, for instance, at 7:30 A.M., I was lying in my hospital bed and I thought, I've just got to talk to that plastic surgeon of mine and find out what we are going to do. He had been off since I became ill and his partner didn't seem to want to commit himself to a decision. I felt like I was being strung along the whole weekend. If the implants were to come out, I wanted them out now. As I reached for the telephone to call Dr. Jim, I glanced out my door and there he was in the flesh.

An hour later Kevin called after he arrived at work and asked me to read a part of the Bible: James 5:13–16. I will quote it now: "Is anyone among you in trouble? He should pray. Is anyone unhappy? He should sing praises. Is there anyone who is sick? He should send for the church elders, who will pray for him and rub olive oil on him in the name of the Lord. This prayer made in faith will heal the sick person; the Lord will restore him to health, and the sins he has committed will be forgiven." I thought, I have things to do but it certainly wouldn't "hurt" me to sit here and do a little biblical reading. As I was finishing the verse, this elderly lady showed up at my door. She was from a Catholic Church and had come to pray and to give me Holy Communion. She didn't have any olive oil to rub, but boy when she left, I kept right on reading that Bible!

The charge nurse tonight is obese and I'm thinking dumb. I'm ashamed of myself for stereotyping fat and dumb together. Intellectually I know this is wrong, but I'm scared. If I had a medical emergency tonight I don't think I'm in competent hands. All my doctors have gone home. If I croak, no one will save me. Isn't that sad; if the charge nurse was prettier and thinner, I might feel more confident when she says that I'm fine. I'd be lucky even to get the station secretary to answer my light. And I have a headache.

Oh, where is that nurse I dream of who has been on this floor for the past fifteen, ten, or even five years? I know they exist somewhere. I worked with two at the old Abbott Hospital in Minneapolis. Linda and Marilene, where are you?

Mary, the charge nurse, just came in and talked with me. I've been so unfair to her. She is obese, but she is also intelligent and kind. I'm sorry. One more emotion for the day—paranoia. I'm so tired that I must go to sleep now. . . .

Tuesday, November 1, proved to be a better day. I was discharged from the Ritz Medical Center. Kevin was busy at work, so I called my friend, Alice, to pick me up from the hospital and bring me home. She said she'd arrive about 12:30 P.M. I was so happy to be leaving. I remember hustling about my hospital room, trying to eat my lunch and collect my belongings at the same time. I felt like I was checking out of a hotel and was trying to take all the extra soaps and complimentary, miscellaneous items. On the wall there was a beautiful, framed picture of a hot air balloon in flight. When Alice arrived I was in the process of eyeballing that picture to determine if it would fit in my suitcase. My first response to Alice was, "Those drugs must really be affecting me; I was actually contemplating stealing that picture!" We began to laugh. If laughter is the best medicine, Alice is the cure for me; she has a crazy sense of humor that I can relate to and enjoy.

I already had a wheelchair in my room, so the next step in my release was to round up my nurse. When the nurse arrived I asked her if I had to ride down in the wheelchair for the discharge procedure. Because she was new with the hospital, she hesitated in answering. While she contemplated, but before she could answer, I piled my belongings into the chair and we were on our way with me pushing my wheelchair, accompanied by the nurse and Alice. Alice and I were giggling like young girls and the poor nurse didn't quite understand the humor in the situation.

I'm not sure what there was to laugh about, but we laughed all the way to my house. Alice and I were both newcomers to the K.C. area, and decided that since we'd started in Missouri, with our destination in Kansas, driving due west would get us there. Wrong—we got lost! Alice was in awe of the colors in the autumn leaves that covered the trees, and I was in awe of how she could admire the leaves and drive at the same time. I arrived home safely and was thankful that Alice was my friend. I remember thinking that I must have been the happiest oncological patient around.

Dorothy Grand

THE FIRST INDICATION that God was actually looking out for me was the arrival of Dorothy Grand at my door. I truly believe that she is an angel that God sent to help me.

Everything that happened in the previous two months had been so ironic. While I was planning the move to Kansas, several nurses at work teased me that I was moving to Kansas to live with Dorothy and Toto. Well, I certainly found Dorothy, but she doesn't have a dog.

It's no miracle how Dorothy found me. A mother in my kindergartner's carpool told a neighbor who knew Dorothy and told Dorothy what had happened. Dorothy heard about this poor young mother who was new to Kansas and had just been diagnosed with breast cancer. She decided to make me her mission; she wanted to be my "Kansas City Mother."

Dorothy and I became immediate soul mates. She is a cute, gray-haired, sixty-six-year-old widow, and a retired nurse. Cancer was not a new subject for her; she had had a mastectomy five years before and her thirty-eight-year-old daughter had undergone mastectomies in the previous year.

To be honest, at first I was a little skeptical of this kind, older lady. Why would someone take *me* on as their mission out of the kindness of her heart? I thought, Maybe she needed the money and would charge us for child care, but she has refused to take payment from us! When I told my father about Dorothy, he was also skeptical; however, when he came to visit I was glad he had the opportunity to meet her. I wanted my father to know that there really were beautiful people in the world, or at least in Kansas. Dorothy has filled many needs for my family—primarily the childrens' needs. She has filled the role of pseudo-grandmother and they call her "Grandma Dorothy."

This lady is a character and a story-teller, much like I am. Dorothy possesses sixty-six years of wisdom. She says her initials, D.G., stand for dumb girl, but she is wrong; this lady is very smart. The other description she coined for herself was "General Grant"; this is much more accurate.

I learned a lot from Dorothy in a short time. She told me about her husband, Eddy, and his death, and the out-of-body experience he had. It was a beautiful story and I believed every word of it. I think it's worth repeating:

Eddy had been hospitalized with congestive heart failure. At about 1:45 A.M., one Sunday, he suffered a cardiac arrest. A medical team attempted to resuscitate him for about twenty minutes before calling Dorothy. When Dorothy and her daughter arrived in Eddy's room the resuscitative efforts were still in progress. It struck Dorothy as a little unusual that they would continue to work so long on a sixty-two-year-old man with a poor prognosis. She thought that once the formality of getting her there was over, the doctor would discontinue resuscitation efforts.

Dorothy put her hand on Eddy's ankle and said, "It's okay, Eddy." At that moment Eddy sat straight up in bed and said, "Wow, was I ever having a dream!" He then proceeded to arrest again. The resuscitative efforts began again while Dorothy sat in a corner of the room, praying Hail Marys.

Eddy's heart started beating again so they put him on a respirator and moved him to the Cardiac Unit. He started chewing on the respirator tube which was helping him to breathe, so the doctor removed it and he was able to breathe on his own. By 10:00 A.M. that Sunday, Eddy was awake and able to correctly identify his family.

On that November evening, at 6:45 P.M., with Dorothy sitting by Eddy's bedside, holding his hand, they had a conversation and it went something like this:

Eddy:	Dorothy, I'm sorry, I must leave you, but it is so peaceful here.
Dorothy:	Eddy, are you in heaven?
Eddy:	Why, of course.
Dorothy:	Have you seen your family?
Eddy:	Yes, and yours too.
Dorothy:	Is Marshall there? [Eddy's deceased brother]
Eddy:	Yes, everyone is here.
Dorothy:	Did you talk to Marshall?
Eddy:	Yes.
Dorothy:	And what did he say?
Eddy:	To tell everyone Hi.

Dorothy and Eddy's daughters were also in the room and they started to question their father.

Pat:	Did you see the bright light?
Eddy:	Oh, yes, it was really bright. It is so beautiful and peaceful here, you can't imagine.
Kay:	And are there angels?
Eddy:	Oh, everywhere. They sing; everyone sings here.
Mary:	How did you get to heaven?
Eddy:	An angel was waiting for me at 90th and Providence. (That is the address of the hospital.)
Kay:	Did you see the Lord?
Eddy:	Yes.
Kay:	What did He say?
Eddy:	Glad you're here.

The family felt they had an opportunity most people on earth don't get to experience—a glimpse of heaven. As Dorothy puts it, "a peek of heaven from around the corner."

Eddy had not been dreaming; he was alert and oriented during this conversation. The nurses heard about the experience and came into Eddy's room to ask him questions. The conversations went something like this:

Nurse:	Eddy, do you know who I am?
Eddy:	Yes, you're Anne.
Nurse:	Have you seen Mr. Floyd? [Her deceased husband]
Eddy:	Yes, but I haven't talked with him yet.

The following day Eddy asked Dorothy what year it was; she told him it was 1980. Eddy insisted that it was 1987. He died a few days later, and as much as Dorothy loved him, she accepted his death and knew that he was in a better place. Dorothy felt that something significant would happen in 1987; she thought it might be the year she would join Eddy in heaven. Dorothy didn't die in 1987, but that was the year her daughter was diagnosed with cancer.

Dorothy is a volunteer worker in a hospice. Many people fear death, and she tries to change their perception by telling them her "glimpse of heaven." Instead of fearing death, we should look forward to it, but that can be so difficult.

There is one other story that Dorothy told me that I will share because it is a lesson. It was a hospital situation that she encountered while she worked as a registered nurse.

Dorothy was the head nurse on an OB-GYN ward. She had an eighty-year-old female patient who was dying of breast cancer. The woman's son-in-law was the mayor in that area and thought he deserved special treatment due to his status. Dorothy's nutshell description of this man was "arrogant and cheap."

Mr. Mayor wanted one-on-one nursing care for his mother-in-law, which meant a nurse on duty for her alone. When he confronted Dorothy with his request, she explained that there were other seriously ill patients on the ward and that she did not have adequate staffing to provide private nursing for his mother-in-law.

Mr. Mayor wanted the hospital to provide the care, but he did not want to spend his money. He became frustrated and yelled at Dorothy, "Goddammit, you think you know it all."

The hospital was a Catholic institution, and after Mr. Mayor's complaint, Dorothy was called before the supervising nun to discuss the conflict.

The nun asked Dorothy if she'd at any time used profanity in her discussion with the Mayor. Dorothy was confused and asked the nun to be a little more specific.

The nun asked, "Did you use any words like shit or damn?"

Dorothy shot back with, "Hell, no. I don't use profanity!"

Dorothy dealt with her frustration with the mayor situation by cutting out a picture of him from the newspaper and placing it on her pin cushion. That way, everytime she sewed, she stuck pins right through his face! I love it, Dorothy! And, I love you.

Dorothy and I shared our feelings on how difficult nursing could be at times, especially times when we were expected to treat patients and families with respect, no matter how rudely they may have acted. My observations are that this is a problem in situations where service is provided.

I shared the following "Susan Exercises Restraint" story with Dorothy: The Transitional Nursery at Minneapolis Childrens' Hospital Medical Center was located in the heart of the city. Consequently, we had experienced many sad occasions when we knew we were sending those beautiful babies home to undesirable, social situations. I believe, as nurses, we really did try to show everyone the same respect; the unmarried mother of three as well as the wealthy, married mother having her first child.

Anyway, a young mother had a Caesarean section and produced a premature baby boy. I was caring for the premie who was in an isolette in the nursery, and the mother had been wheeled into the nursery to see her baby. She didn't look too chipper and seemed to be in pain. The father followed behind her, wearing a hat with printing on it that said, "Life's a bitch, then you marry one." I couldn't believe this guy would have the gall to wear that hat to the hospital where his wife had just delivered his child. Although my instinct was to stomp on that hat with both feet, I was kind and courteous to that new daddy!

The second angel to enter my life was a delightful lady by the name of Lynn. She had a daughter in the same classroom at school as my oldest daughter.

Lynn had heard about my impending mastectomies and called me the night before surgery. What struck me initially about her was her strong belief in God. She called to tell me that a prayer chain was going to be started for me in the morning, and that by the time surgery was over, the greater part of Kansas City would be praying for me. *For me!* Lynn's call made me realize just how much support was out there for me.

In the course of our conversation, Lynn and I discovered a few coincidences; she was also a nurse and worked in the same unit at St. Joseph's Hospital where I had been hired to work.

The head nurse had told Lynn that she had just hired a new nurse for the unit who reminded her of Lynn. Later on, Lynn asked the nurse the whereabouts of the new nurse and was told that something had come up and the new nurse wouldn't be able to start as planned. We concluded that I was that nurse. Another coincidence was that both of our husbands worked at Marion Laboratories. The last, sad coincidence was that we had both lost our mothers to cancer.

My first impression of Lynn was that she was too nice. I felt a little bit intimidated by her, and was reluctant to let the real me come out. The words "shit" and "damn" had become ingrained in my vocabulary, and I didn't feel comfortable using them in Lynn's presence. As I got to really know Lynn, I learned that she was very non-judgmental and accepted people as they were. It didn't take me long to be able to say, "Lynn, this is a damn, shitty situation!" I knew she would understand.

Lynn is a beautiful person inside and outside. She has wide, sincere eyes that would never lie. She was so optimistic that I was cured; she truly believed it. Occasionally she accompanied me when I received my chemotherapy and we'd go out for lunch afterwards. We always laughed and had a good time together; she has a marvelous sense of humor, faith in God, and belief in me. She is the kind of person I need to surround myself with. When I told her that my prognosis was 80 percent for beating the cancer, she replied, "Yes, but the Holy Spirit is kicking in the other 20 percent!" Lynn radiated the Spirit, and I don't doubt her.

Jane was the third angel God delivered to me; it was another coincidental meeting. In August, we were walking from church after Sunday mass and Kevin noticed a mini-van with Minnesota license plates parked in front of our mini-van. A man, woman, and three young boys were approaching the mini-van and they were about to climb into their vehicle. My instinct normally would have been to think, Isn't that nice; they're from Minnesota too. I would have ignored them unless they approached me first. Kevin, on the other hand, approached them and introduced himself and our family. Jane and Steve Carlson, along with their three young boys had also just moved to Kansas. Our son Paul and their oldest son ended up in the same classroom in school and also were placed on the same soccer team. Jane and Steve's middle son was on our daughter's soccer team.

Jane Carlson appointed herself to be my childrens' personal taxi service when I was hospitalized and later, while I recuperated. We lived in the same vicinity and she would pick up the children for soccer practices, games, birthday parties, etc. I desperately wanted my childrens' lives to continue to be as normal as possible without my illness disrupting their activities. Jane was a major factor in helping to keep the kids' lives on an even keel. It was a constant amazement to me that whenever there was a need, the need was filled by "angels."

One decision that we faced when we'd learned we were moving to Kansas was whether to send our children to the public school (three blocks from our new home), or bus them to the Catholic school that was five miles away. Kevin wanted them to attend the Catholic school and I was leaning towards sending them to the public school, mainly for convenience sake. Our final decision was to send them to Cure of Ars Catholic School. Having them in a Catholic learning environment was really not a big issue with me;

however, I was glad the children were enrolled in a school in which God was spoken of freely.

I don't know what the response would have been had the children attended the public school, but the response to my illness at Cure, once my diagnosis spread, was overwhelming. Our family was embraced with much love and support. Even during the midst of our crisis, I believed that if my life would be spared, I would be able to look back someday and say that it had all been a positive experience. It was wonderful for my children to have experienced such a giving community.

Besides calls of support and prayers, the mothers in my childrens' classes started a meals program for us. What a lifesaver! My next door neighbor's Bible study group also did the same thing. For three weeks straight, starting the day I had my mastectomy surgery, dinners were delivered to our home. Some days we got two and three meals. Besides being well nourished, our empty freezer was filled. With my recuperation, the emotional upheaval and the out-of-state company, there was no energy for meal preparation. This helped tremendously. The only problem the dinners presented for me was potential embarrassment; by the end of three weeks, I had recouped enough to start running again and I was afraid that while running, I would be spotted by someone driving to my house with a meal. I envisioned them thinking, *That's* the invalid I've just cooked for?

Another support person who appeared at our front door was Father Thomas Tank, our parish pastor. He came to visit Kevin and I after I was diagnosed with cancer, and just prior to surgery. Father Tank is a gray-haired, middle-aged, rugged-appearing man who looked more like a neighbor you'd have a beer with than a priest. I don't remember any uplifting spiritual insight he had to offer, but he offered the assistance of the parish in any way. At the time of his visit, I was feeling healthy and told Father how uncomfortable it was for us to receive all this help from people, especially people we barely knew; this is where Father Tank's words of wisdom helped. He said it was much easier to give than to receive and that people *want* to help us because it helps *them* feel good. That's true. They couldn't change my cancer diagnosis; however, they could assist in making the rest of our life less stressful. After Father Tank left, I decided it would be okay to sit back and be a receiver for a while, and allow others to feel good.

One Sunday, during a sermon, Father Tank sent me a message on giving. He began with a story illustrating a lesson lost, but for me it was a lesson learned. Here is his story:

> A father, wishing to teach his daughter something about generosity to the Church, one day on the way to mass gave his daughter two coins—a fifty-cent piece and a dime. He told her that she could put either of the coins into the collection basket; it was her decision. When the time came for the collection to be taken, the little girl put her dime in the basket. Her father, a little disappointed, didn't say anything until they were on their way home. He asked her, "Honey, why did you put the dime in the collection rather than the fifty-cent piece?" She responded, "Father said that God loves a cheerful giver and I figured I would be a lot more cheerful if I gave ten cents instead of fifty cents."

That message made me realize that because I had given so little, I was a cheerful giver! Father also went on to say that no matter what we gave, it had to be a true expression of the gratitude we offered to God for His blessings given to us, and of the love that we wished to express to Him and others through the gifts of our resources. I'd received so many blessings and given, comparatively, so little that I felt ashamed. At that Sunday mass, I decided that if my life would be spared from the cancer, I would dedicate the rest of my life on earth to giving more.

Physicians' Wives

UNTIL WE MOVED TO KANSAS, I hadn't personally been acquainted with any physicians' wives. During the course of my nursing career, I'd worked with a lot of physicians and was often curious about their wives. As a nurse, from time to time, I had heard gossip regarding a certain doctor's wife. Although I really never held a stereotyped opinion of doctors' wives, I suppose I thought that they were economically pampered women.

After our arrival in Kansas, it seemed that every other woman with whom I became acquainted was married to a physician. These new associations have changed my view of doctors' wives. The wives I met seem to possess a great deal of character. I'm sure they all have their own stories of the early struggles during the time their husbands were in medical school and, later on, serving their residencies. The economic pampering, perhaps, is earned after a very long time of dedication and tolerance on the part of these women. Interestingly, though, I did notice that upon meeting a physician's wife for the first time, sometime within the first two minutes of conversation, they subtly made me aware that they were married to a doctor.

The first doctor's wife I met was Chris, my next door neighbor. Although Chris's husband, Bob, worked long hours as an Emergency Room physician, I never heard her complain. When I met Chris, it was immediately apparent that she had a very deep Christian faith. She wasn't a "Bible-thumping Holy Roller," but simply a believer and Spirit-filled. I'll never forget the day we arrived at our new home; we were greeted with welcome signs on our front door that Chris and Bob's children had hung there. Chris had prepared an entire meal for our family of six—our first evening meal in our new home. As I got to know these people better, I was impressed by their deep faith, and at the same time, they were such fun people to be with. Chris and I hit it off right away; motherhood was our common venture.

Alice was another physician's wife that I became friends with. Possibly I should have included Alice in the section "Angels God Sent," but Alice is about as angelical as I. Our family arrived in Kansas on July 17; Alice and her family arrived in Kansas on July 27, having relocated from Canton, Ohio. Alice and I met in the school parking lot when we were bringing our kindergartners to their first day of school. Ironically, Alice's husband's specialty was oncology! Her background in spirituality was similar to mine; we had both been burdened with doubting thoughts of God's existence. Alice had also recently experienced a crisis in her life and said to me, "If God would just give us a hint, just a hint, to hang in there and to believe. . . . " A hint was all we were asking for.

Alice gave me a different perspective of life as the wife of a physician. Although her story wasn't typical of all such marriages, I'm sure she wasn't alone. Her crisis had been that she had lived in a marriage that she felt she could no longer tolerate. In Canton, Ohio, where her husband had a thriving oncology practice, their marriage relationship had deteriorated. She was married to a wonderful man who was married to his profession and was very dedicated to his patients. (From a patient's viewpoint, the kind of doctor I'd wanted.) Alice was very lonely and had harbored much anger toward this wonderful, dedicated man whom she loved. There had been too many Thanksgiving dinners and Christmas celebrations missed because he felt he was needed at the hospital with his patients, rather than with his family. In anger, Alice had told him, "In five years those patients won't remember your commitment, but your children will never forget!" She told me that in a situation like theirs had been, since she couldn't physically have him, she'd used the material things he provided. He then viewed her as an object—an object who could be placated with the purchase of more "things."

Alice related one incident regarding a ball put on by the hospital auxiliary at her husband's hospital. Those wives had put on that very elegant ball to honor their husbands, a theme that nearly physically "gagged" her. Alice thought the theme was all wrong; she thought the physicians should have been honoring their wives for all the garbage they'd endured!

Finally, Alice had become so unhappy with her marriage she decided that they either had to change the situation or dissolve the marriage. They'd opted for change and part of that change was moving to Kansas. Her husband had given up his thriving practice to begin a teaching position at a local university which offered regular hours and less commitments.

While our situations were very different, Alice and I had a lot in common and our coping mechanisms were similar. She and I joked that perhaps God was only in Kansas because we both had acquired a stronger faith since moving there, and we felt that God was actually helping us.

Sometimes Alice and I would meet for lunch after my Monday chemotherapy treatments. She would say, "Susan, the normal person just doesn't go out for lunch after chemo." It was her suggestion to name my book *Chemo and Lunch*. During our conversations, I found Alice to be intelligent, humorous, and inspirational. She viewed her marital crisis as the best crisis she'd ever gone through. Although it had been a big risk for them to move from Ohio, Kansas had given them a better life and an opportunity to rebuild a relationship, one that I suspected neither one really wanted to dissolve. Alice used to tell me that if I survived my cancer crisis, it would end up being the best thing that ever happened to me. Alice was right; it had already been a learning experience for me. Alice said, "We're survivors; we're not victims. Victims never climb out of their holes. Alice and Susan are survivors!"

Once during one of our after-chemo-Monday lunches, I confided to Alice that things were going so well for me and that I thought I was much too happy. She told me that the Spirit had elevated me to a state of grace. I hadn't previously thought much about grace; it had seemed like an abstract concept to me. I looked up the definition of "grace"; the dictionary simply stated that grace is "Help given man by God." I do believe that God elevated me into a state of grace, and because my life has been so enriched, I view the world and life differently now.

Another physician's wife who has helped me is Kathy. Our daughters were playing on the same soccer team. My first impression of Kathy was that she was a cheerful, energetic person. When she learned that I had bilateral mastectomies, she called me on my phone with a list of a dozen things she would do in order to help me. She was the only person who offered to clean our house and I took her up on her offer! A week after my surgery, Kathy came over and cleaned the entire house; I was very grateful for her help considering my preconceived ideas regarding physicians' wives. I was surprised that one was actually *cleaning my house!*

Minneapolis Mission

DR. HENRY LYNCH and his team of researchers at the Hereditary Institute at Creighton University in Omaha, Nebraska, had gathered enough information from my relatives' autopsy and medical reports to convince them that this was a family on which they wanted to conduct in-depth research. They have concluded that we are passing a breast-ovarian gene from generation to generation. To further their study and to offer information and education to my relatives, Dr. Lynch and his team planned to go to Minneapolis the weekend of November 11–12, 1988. Appointments were made Saturday and Sunday for conferences with each of the "tree" branches that could and wanted to attend. The team planned to draw blood, take tissue samples, and breast aspirates from designated family members.

I didn't feel I could miss out on the event that I helped to bring about. So, on Friday, November 10, I finished my home course in IV Antibiotics and left on a flight bound for Minneapolis. This was my first trip back home since we'd moved away, nearly four months before; I was so excited I could hardly stand it. Kevin stayed home in Kansas with our children. My two younger sisters planned to meet me at the airport, and when my plane landed at approximately 8:15 P.M., I was expecting a teary-eyed reunion. I had not seen Corinne and Pam since I left Minneapolis. I got off the plane, went to the end of the gate, and no one was there to meet me! I was so hyper, looking around in utter disbelief that no one was there. What I didn't know was that Corinne and Pam were finishing their drinks in a nearby airport bar, watching me in my anxiety attack, and they were laughing. Finally they decided they had better come meet me, giggling to themselves as they approached. They confessed what they had done, and we all three laughed, and continued to laugh for the next hour.

From the airport we drove directly to Maple Lake, Minnesota, where there was a benefit in progress for my cousin, Michael, and his wife. Michael is Aunt Kathryn's son and Aunt Kathryn was in the hospital that weekend experiencing complications from her progressing breast cancer. Michael's wife, Trela, thirty-eight years old, had also received a breast cancer diagnosis the past summer and it had spread to her liver. Michael and Trela had no medical insurance, so the farming community had joined together to raise money for them. I felt sorry for Michael because his mother was dying of breast cancer at the time.

We arrived at the packed, smoke-filled American Legion Post building at 9:30 P.M. With the exception of the casual attire in the room, there was an atmosphere similar to wedding receptions I'd been to in the past. Trela was there and appeared to be doing very well. I had seen her before on a few occasions over the past fifteen years, but this time it was different. We hugged each other and experienced a common bond. Before I had time to think about it, I headed for the stage. The band was on break and a woman was using the microphone, in the process of raffling off some of the donated items. I asked her if I could say a few words and she consented, so I tapped on the microphone until the noise in the room quieted down. If I was ever driven by the Spirit, that was the moment. Suddenly I realized I had a captive audience, and I thought, This better be good! First I told them who I was and gave them a brief history of my diagnosis and mastectomies. I also said that Trela and I had a lot in common; both of us were young mothers with cancer. Then I spoke directly to Trela and said, "Trela, I don't know if I'll be cured, and I don't know if you'll be cured, but there is not one single person in this room who knows if they'll be alive tomorrow. I do, however, believe in the power of prayer. If everyone in this room gives not only their financial contributions to Mike and Trela, but also prays for them, God will give them the strength to endure this crisis!" My message was well received by the audience as they applauded, my family was in tears, and the lady who had relinquished the microphone hugged me. At that moment, I truly felt I was a witness for Christ.

The band played and I spent the rest of the evening dancing with relatives. My father was there for the benefit, and I rode home with him to his house to spend the weekend. I got to sleep at 3:00 A.M.!

On Saturday I had lunch with my oldest and dearest friend, Rose. We laughed for two hours, reminisced about our childhood and discussed the challenges of motherhood. For the first time in our twenty-eight-year friendship, we talked about our faith in God. I thought I knew Rose so well, but I had been unaware of her deep faith. It made me sad to realize that it had taken my illness to discover Rose's faith.

On Saturday evening I finally got to meet my hero, Dr. Henry Lynch. I was thrilled just to shake his hand. A small dinner party had been planned for that evening with Dr. Lynch and his team, which consisted of three nurses, one of which was his wife, Jane. Also present was Dr. John Potter from the University of Minnesota and his wife. Dr. Potter, an associate professor and epidemiology director in cancer research, was researching environmental factors and their relationship to cancer.

Dr. Lynch, a tall man in his sixties, towered over me. His personality and smile were heart-warming. He wanted to hear the story of my trials with my cancer diagnosis; he and his team listened intently. They not only listened, but they cared, and most of all they understood. Dr. Lynch was excited to have my family as part of his research. He had studied over a thousand families with suspected hereditary cancer, but had never tracked a family as large as ours. We have the distinction of being one of the largest hereditary cancer families in the United States.

I bluntly asked Dr. Lynch if he was going to gather information and samples from relatives, return to Creighton, write up a report, and then simply forget about us. He assured me that he would never forget us and would be a continual resource to us. My concern was primarily for my three daughters and their future. Dr. Lynch sympathetically told me that he could not guarantee anything; however, with the advances in molecular genetics during the last few years, there is the hope of a breakthrough. They hope to isolate the gene or find the chemical markers in blood that will tell which individuals are at risk for cancer. If this should happen, he said they would call me and make arrangements to have my girls tested. All of that specialized research, however, is dependent on funding and whether or not the team continued to function. That's a lot of "ifs" but nevertheless it gave me some much-needed hope for my daughters.

I feel strongly that I was genetically programmed to contract cancer at age thirty-two, yet there remains some lingering guilt on what I may have done to "cause" the cancer to develop. Perhaps, somehow I sparked that ominous gene. I discussed the subject with Dr. Potter, honestly confessing the environmental insults I'd forced on my body. I'd smoked cigarettes as an adolescent and young adult. Dr. Potter told me that there was no known correlation between smoking and breast cancer. I questioned him regarding the new studies associating alcohol consumption and breast cancer and he said that studies had shown a moderate increase in the risk of breast cancer with alcohol compared with the risk for nondrinkers. Yet, there is no compelling biological explanation for the association. My last question was whether caffeine had some significance in breast cancer because as a college student and night nurse I'd consumed a lot of it. Dr. Potter said there was no proven correlation. I think he was being honest when he told me that he felt that with my age and my family history, the gene was ready to express itself. I felt better, but will always wonder if I hadn't somehow sparked that gene myself. No one will ever know for sure.

I learned a lot from Drs. Lynch and Potter that evening. For instance, I had been living with the misconception that by running and carrying a low body fat, I was lowering my risk. Also, I had always heard that bearing children at a young age and breast feeding lowered the risk of breast cancer. They told me that those factors were only in regard to post-menopausal breast cancer and have no relevance in pre-menopausal, genetic cancer. That was news to me; it really proved to be an evening of enlightenment for me.

One Sunday morning my sister, Pam, my father, and I went to the hospital to visit Aunt Kathryn. I knew that it would be the last time I would see her alive. She looked like a seventy-five year old although she was only sixty years old. She was a tough lady, and recognized each one of us. It made me sad to think that maybe she could have been cured by the conventional, American medicine that she'd shunned for so long.

Aunt Kathryn was still actively involved in a desperate mission to save herself. In her hospital room she had a cigar box containing ampules of vaccines she'd purchased in Japan. The physicians and nurses who were caring for her respected her need to medicate herself. Aunt Kathryn asked me if I would give her a shot from her box of what I considered "voodoo medicine." Her request startled me; as a nurse, it went against my grain to give an unordered, unknown medicine to a patient. My first thought was, If a nurse were to walk in and see me, I could lose my license. Just as quickly, I thought, What the hell, I don't even have a Minnesota nursing license, and who here even knows that I'm a nurse? Because of my hesitation, Aunt Kathryn drew some of the mysterious vaccine into a syringe and said that she'd inject it herself if I wasn't going to do it. I gave her the shot. Thinking retrospectively, I guess that was my way of expressing my approval of her doing something she believed in. I respected her right to do that, but also I felt that she'd chosen the wrong route.

Following that visit to Aunt Kathryn's hospital room, my "branch" of the family tree had our appointment with Dr. Lynch and his team at a nearby medical building. The family group consisted of my brother, sisters, father, and many of our cousins, some of whom had flown in from out of state. It was exciting for me to see my long sought after dream becoming a reality. First we had a conference with Dr. Lynch and then blood samples for the research were taken. Questions were asked and answered; it was an educational experience for everyone. Basically, the females were told they were at 50 percent risk of carrying this autosomal dominant breast/ovarian cancer gene. Dr. Lynch made suggestions regarding prophylactic measures, such as having ovaries removed after childbearing was completed. With so many members of the family present, I felt that my early cancer diagnosis had prompted my young cousins to become interested in the research and, thus, were made aware of their own health risks.

During the conference I asked Dr. Lynch his opinion on why our physicians hadn't listened to us. My sisters, ages twenty-five, twenty-nine, and thirty-four had been told that they didn't need mammograms yet. He explained that only approximately ten percent of cancers are hereditary and that those doctors simply lacked the knowledge regarding hereditary patients and that their approach should have been different. For instance, in cases where hereditary cancer is a factor, diagnostic tests should be started at an earlier age and done more frequently than for the general population.

Dr. Lynch really gave me a wonderful compliment when he compared me to Ignes Semmelweis, a physician in the mid-1800s who told other physicians to wash their hands between patients to prevent infections. In Dr. Semmelweis' time, physicians would go from one childbearing mother to the next, without washing in-between. Because there was very little knowledge of micro-organisms then, Semmelweis was considered to be a little bit crazy because of his suggestion. Nowadays, the washing of hands is considered the most effective method of preventing infections. Dr. Lynch said, "You, Susan, are the present-day Semmelweis." When I had been screaming that cancer was headed "our" way, no one really listened to me, but Dr. Lynch understood. Actually *he* is the present-day Semmelweis; he has been studying familial cancer for twenty-five years, and initially people thought he was crazy, too.

Dr. Lynch's perception of the Hereditary Cancer Institute was that its role was to educate and update physicians on new research findings. The institute planned to send a letter to all the female family members' physicians with the information that they did, indeed, have a patient who was 50 percent at risk of expressing the breast/ovarian cancer gene, and what preventative measures could/should be taken.

During that weekend, my thoughts often were centered on what my father must have been thinking. We all had observed how difficult it had been for my grandfather to have witnessed his wife and several daughters dying of cancer. My father has five daughters, and I am worried that history may repeat itself. Dr. Lynch talked directly to my father on that subject, and said it was a toss of the coin, a fifty-fifty chance. Optimistically he said, "Susan may be your only daughter to develop cancer; you may have two out of five, or five out of five, but again, Susan, may be the only one."

My flight back to Kansas City left Minneapolis at 2:35 P.M., Sunday afternoon. Dr. Lynch and his team were at the airport at the same time; their flight scheduled to leave for Omaha at almost the same time as mine. Our paths crossed at the airport and we hugged each other as we exchanged "thank-yous" and "good-byes." I left Minneapolis knowing my cancer diagnosis had served a purpose. I felt like somewhat of a hero for beginning the project two and a half years previously, by tracing my family tree. I had no desire to be a dead hero—it was a bittersweet victory! I got to witness yet another miracle in my life that weekend; my Northwest flight actually landed in Kansas City ten minutes *early*. Kevin and our four children were waiting for me at the gate.

Sex and Other Post-Mastectomy Miscellaneous

I DID NOT EXPERIENCE a reoccurrence of the breast implant infection and resumed my weekly chemotherapy treatments and frequent visits to the plastic surgeon for breast reconstruction. Although we felt that we had come through the worst of the ordeal, my cancer diagnosis continued to hover over us. As much as we longed to establish normalcy, we soon came to the realization that our lives would be altered for a long time to come. Cancer was always on our minds; I'd wake up in the morning and my first thought would be cancer. I'd think about it driving in the van, and it would be my last thought before falling asleep at night. No matter how hard I tried to erase the cancer thoughts from my mind, I couldn't. There were so many constant reminders: the weekly chemotherapy treatments, the PIC line in my arm, and my appearance. I prayed that someday it would all be a part of our past.

The seven weeks while I was taking Prednisone were especially trying for Kevin. The side effects were much the same as the effects of speed, and from my perspective, it was both great and awful at the same time. I had to constantly calm myself down, but I accomplished more, both physically and mentally, than ever before. I was only able to sleep about four hours each night, and I'd be wide awake at 3:00 A.M., my mind constantly thinking. Prednisone is used in the treatment of many diseases and is considered an antineoplastic (anti-cancer) drug, also. I don't believe that! I think I was put on Prednisone so that I could get my life back in order. I was fearful I would experience depression when the time came to wean me from the drug, and although that didn't happen, life didn't look quite the same. I think everyone should be on Prednisone!

About half-way through my chemotherapy schedule, I did experience a mini-mid-winter depression; my positive attitude faded and anger began to surface. The weekly clinic visits got real old and I resented the time and money we were forced to invest in my health. I remember leaving the clinic in tears one day because I was mad at the nurse. She'd never asked me how I was and didn't respond much to my complaint about my sore knee. Her suggestion was to "quit running." As I drove home, I thought, Doesn't she realize how important exercise is for me? No, she's overweight, and she's probably jealous. I could have thrown up my guts all week long and she wouldn't have cared. I'm just another case to them, but this is still major to *me!* You would think for the $70 they charge to inject chemo into my line, that I could get a simple "How are you?" and "Do you have any problems that I should relay to the doctor?" I could inject the damn chemo into my veins myself and it would save $70! Actually, the nurses at the clinic were very nice to me, but I was very sensitive.

Another angry time was when I was sitting in the laboratory waiting area, waiting for my name to be called for them to draw blood from me. The room was filled with very old people, most likely cancer patients. I looked at all of them and they seemed so sickly and sad. I had an urge to stand up and yell at them, "You're damn lucky you made it to the age you are before getting cancer! You've lived long lives, and you have grown children and grandchildren—you shouldn't be so sad!" The disparity in their ages and mine angered me. In retrospect, I really didn't experience a lot of anger, although it surfaced occasionally.

Thankfully, I was feeling good and I tolerated the chemotherapy extremely well. I was never "sick," not even a cold during the winter. People were amazed at how well I was doing; I was not the stereotypic chemotherapy patient, which was a blessing.

The only side effect I experienced from the chemo was hair loss. I thought that I was psychologically prepared for it, but found it devastating nonetheless. It was slow torture—a gradual thinning. I was glad to be feeling so well, and although I knew the hair loss would be temporary, it still depressed me. I couldn't believe how much of my self-esteem was attached to that hair that floated down the drain. I was trying to perceive myself as healthy, but found it difficult when I looked like a "cancer victim." It irritated me that vanity was still a part of my well-being and I was envious of women with nice hair. Even though Kevin encouraged me to buy a wig, I didn't because I was more self-conscious about wearing a wig that looked like a wig. I finally resorted to wearing a scarf.

Even though I didn't lose all the hair on my head, it became thin and unsightly. The whole process was much more difficult for me than I'd ever anticipated. The hair that remained continued to grow, and I finally decided that I needed to get whatever hair that I had left, cut. I went to a "walk-in," cut-rate shop and had to wait forty minutes for my turn. As I waited, I had time to think about how the young, female beautician would react to my balding scalp when I took off the scarf. Judgmental thoughts filled my head. I thought, I'll just blow her away because she'll never be able to relate to someone my age with cancer. Finally, when my name was called, I sat down in the chair and took off my scarf. I quickly explained to the girl that was about to cut my hair that I didn't have much to cut because I had been on chemotherapy. She very nonchalantly responded that she had lost her hair six years previously when she'd undergone radiation treatment. Her statement blew *me* away! She told me that she'd had breast cancer at age twenty-five and also had silicone implants. It was good for me to be reminded that I'm just one of many young women with breast cancer. It was also good to meet another survivor.

The reconstruction process of my breasts was more involved than I had anticipated. The plastic surgeon injected fluid into those knobs that were under my skin, on each side of my chest. The knobs had tubes that led to the implants, the fluid gradually enlarging the implants in order to stretch muscle and skin. I got to my desired size and was looking rather well. The next step was for the surgeon to continue inflating the implants. He said that the larger he would make the capsule, the better the final silicone would look when implanted. I would rather have had no breasts than those "things" that looked and felt like two oversized grapefruits under my skin; I lost any desire I'd ever had to be large busted! I actually closed doors on those newly acquired pseudobreasts. One day when cleaning the mini-van, I actually got lodged between the seat and steering wheel because of the large implants. Discomfort lasted for about twenty-four hours after Dr. Jim inflated them because the chest muscles were stretched. I referred to that awful feeling as "chest labor." Then I had to walk around with a grapefruit chest on my petite frame for three months! When it was winter I was thankful that I could hide under sweaters.

It was to be a long winter. Aunt Kathryn finally died from breast cancer in January. Her Christmas card to me got lost in the mail and I received it after her funeral. That winter my maternal grandmother's cousin's daughter was diagnosed with ovarian cancer. She was one of the people I'd telephoned when I first began working on the family tree. For her sake and mine, I should have started the research five years sooner.

As spring approached, I became impatient to get finished with the chemo. Patience is what I needed and never had an abundance of. I found myself wishing away time and longed for it to be summer. The plan was to finish chemo in May, and to have a total hysterectomy and have the silicone implanted in June.

My winter depression had lifted, but in early spring I began experiencing pain in my left hip; the mental battle was on. After a week and a half of the hip pain, I was convinced that the cancer had spread to my bones. I began to question exactly how much control I actually had over the disease. I wouldn't have given a second thought to the discomfort, had I not had cancer. But, as it was, I no longer believed that I'd been healed and insisted on another bone scan. Before the results came back, I'd chosen a "casket dress" and made Kevin promise to tell the girls about their periods. The bone scan was negative, the hip pain disappeared, and optimism was back in my life. It did upset me, though, that I had let doubt consume me to such a degree.

My hair started to grow back before I had finished with my chemotherapy. I thought I was looking pretty good in April, so I quit wearing the scarf around the house. I guess I didn't look *that* good and must have still had the appearance of a cancer patient, because one day a lady at the door said, "By the looks of you, I bet you're going through what I've been through." This lady was probably in her mid-fifties. After I confirmed her suspicion, she proceeded to tell me in detail of her experience with breast cancer. She was very kind and I know she was really trying to empathize with me, but again, the disparity in our ages was a problem for me. She commented that she would like to live long enough to see her youngest child reach age thirty-five. With a smile on my face I thought, Lady, *I'd* like to see thirty-five! I'd like to see my children through grade school! When she left, I didn't know whether to laugh or cry.

My sister called that month to tell me that my cousin Sandy, age thirty, went to Rochester, Minnesota and had bilateral mastectomies and a total hysterectomy purely to prevent cancer. I guess with her mother having cancer and then me being diagnosed at age thirty-two, Sandy wasn't going to take any chances. Intellectually I thought Sandy had done the right thing, but when my sister first told me, my initial reaction was, "Wow, that was a rather drastic move!" When they removed my cousin's left breast, they found a 0.8 tumor that was cancerous! Drastic perhaps, but prudent. Sandy's lymph nodes were clean but she is still undergoing a course of chemotherapy.

I was happy for Sandy because I really believe what she did in the long-run will prove to be a life-saver. Her surgery and cancer diagnosis, however, was a sad reminder to me of what I should have done when I was thirty. I know if I would have had the prophylactic mastectomies then, they would have found my cancer. If it was only 0.8 cms when I was thirty, it certainly wouldn't have metastasized to my lymph nodes. If only we could turn the clock back. Yes, I should have done what Sandy did. If only, if only . . .

May also brought sad news. My dad called to tell me that Trela had died of breast cancer. She had only been diagnosed one year previously and now she was dead. I think people were concerned about my reaction to her death, but actually I dealt with it okay. I felt sad for Michael and his children, but knew that even though Trela and I both had the same disease, it didn't necessarily mean the outcome would be the same.

May was over and so was my chemotherapy; I was done! In late June, I had a total abdominal hysterectomy and silicone breast implants at the same time. I recovered quickly and started to make big plans for the coming year. The past year had been consumed with my health; I wanted to shelve the cancer, as a chapter of my past. Now I'd have time to pursue normal activities.

Oh, but this cancer won't go away. It continues to grow throughout my family tree. Another telephone call in July informed me that my sister Dolly, age thirty-five, was diagnosed with breast cancer. I had no tears left to cry. I just wanted to scream in frustration. Now I must support my sister.

I had prayers, angels sent from God, a sense of humor, excellent physicians, friends, and family to help me cope with my diagnosis. That was wonderful, but the most significant factor in my recovery was Kevin's continual support and love. He showed me what true marital commitment was all about and exhibited a strength that I'd not previously recognized in him. From the very beginning, Kevin said, "We are going to beat this thing, together!" While I was the recipient of an unbelievable amount of attention, Kevin was crumbling inside. This ordeal has been much harder on him than on me, but he never complained. Through all of it I was assured of his love for me, and with such love, I felt very, very fortunate.

We were often riding an emotional roller coaster. Kevin would usually have to cheer me up, but occasionally I'd have to pick him up. Christmas was especially difficult. Kevin was videotaping the children and me while we decorated the tree and he had to leave the room because he became choked up. He was thinking, How many Christmases will we have together as a family? It was times like that when I'd say, "Hey, I've beat it!" The most overwhelming emotion to deal with, for both of us, was fear.

The one thing we did plan together as a family was my Five Year Cure Party and our fifteenth wedding anniversary celebration. The children had fun trying to figure out how old they would be, and I promised them there would be dancing clowns. I made Kevin promise that there would be champagne-filled fountains—not the cheap stuff we'd had at our wedding reception! Our oldest daughter contributed some reality into our planning by saying, "Mom, you're dreaming!" I told her she was right, but that I'd had dreams come true before.

Is there a sex life after a mastectomy? Yes. I remember my feelings as I laid in the hospital bed the day after the mastectomies. I looked down at the bandages that covered my mutilated chest and, although I was confident of Kevin's love for me, I feared that he would begin to love me more as a sister than as a wife. I cried and cried, thinking that our intimate relationship was over, but I was wrong. I had attached too much importance to the rôle of breasts in sexuality. Kevin still needed me as desperately as I needed him. His acceptance of my balding scalp and pseudo-breasts made it easier for me to accept my altered form.

We had been in our new home for over three months and had not taken the opportunity to bathe together in our oversized bath tub. We'd thought about it, but we never got around to it. One Saturday evening, three weeks post-mastectomy, the children all asleep, Kevin and I found ourselves alone for the first time. It seemed like ages since we'd been alone; the atmosphere was ripe for a romantic encounter. I filled the bath tub with warm water and bubbles and Kevin poured two glasses of champagne. As we undressed to climb into the tub together, I realized that I still had the PIC line in my arm and that it couldn't get wet. I wasn't about to let that damn PIC line ruin our evening, so I got a box of kitchen plastic wrap and Kevin wrapped my arm, protecting the PIC line. We proceeded into the tub, although I had to hold my arm out of the water. Somewhere in the process, a lot of the romance was lost and it hardly seemed worth all the effort. But, I guess it was worth the effort—we were able to laugh about the scenario later on.

Kevin's love and support were always there, but I also had to help myself. As a child, I remember hearing my mother say, "The Lord helps those who help themselves." I knew that I couldn't rely completely on outside forces for my recovery; some of it had to come from within me.

So what did I do for myself? I refused to feel sorry for myself (which wasn't always easy). My father said, "A sick mind dwells on the past; a healthy mind looks forward." I wouldn't dwell on the "what ifs." I had the choice of viewing myself as a victim or a survivor. Alice said I was a survivor, and that's the route I chose. I prayed for strength, read books on mental attitude and courage, and hung notes on positive points on my bathroom mirror. Occasionally I lapsed into doubt, but, for the most part, I believed I was cured.

Diet is important when undergoing chemotherapy. While the drugs destroy the cancer cells, they also destroy healthy cells in the body. I tried to eat a high protein diet which helps to repair the cells. Drinking a lot of water is also important because fluids protect the kidneys from the harsh drugs and help to flush out dead cancer cells. Wine was the one fluid I allowed myself to drink, although it clearly was a contradiction to therapy and soon ended when my liver enzymes went wacko. Water became very boring!

I religiously took my medication and went every Monday for IV chemotherapy. Twice a day I took the anti-cancer drug, Cytoxin. Along with Cytoxin, I added a multi-vitamin, iron, and vitamin C. My white blood count was often way below normal, but I remained healthy.

Exercise became more important to me than ever. I looked like a chemo patient, but I sure didn't want to feel like one. Mentally and physically, exercise was vital. I began calisthenics which helped my entire body, but especially strengthened my arm muscles and helped me to regain mobility in my arms following the mastectomies. Running became more important to me than ever before; I needed to perceive my body's condition as a healthy one, and running was a way to prove it to myself, over and over. Running was my way of saying, "Cancer, up yours!"

My Children

LIFE IS SO IRONIC SOMETIMES. My ovaries and breasts, the parts of my body that made it possible to conceive and nourish my babies, now threaten my life. They also threaten my children's future, a possibility of growing up motherless. My children have been the most difficult aspect of my cancer diagnosis for me to deal with. It rips at my heart to think that I *could* die and leave them. *I can't leave my babies!* I know, all too well, how irreplaceable a mother's love is. When my mother died, my younger sister was only seven years old, and it has always disturbed me that Pam has such little memory of the woman who gave birth to her. My children are so young; they need me. I will not be a faded memory to them, a speck in their past. There are days when it hurts too much to even look at their beautiful faces. There are days when I want to hug them forever.

I have three daughters and one son, and I carry the guilt of bearing these girls and passing them the risk of carrying this breast/ovarian cancer gene. Why did I have so many girls? If I had known a decade ago what I know now, I would not have produced four children. I worry for my daughters' future and feel very guilty.

When we had the children, I wanted to give them family names so that they would have "roots." Sadly, I now realize that all my daughters are named after cancer victims. My oldest, Kathryn Elda, was named after my mother Elda. Bridget Mary was named after my godmother, Aunt Mary. And my baby, Maureen Susan, is named after me. I pray that the cancer gene wasn't passed to them along with their names!

Kathryn, age eight, is a kind, sensitive child. I made Kevin promise to hire a nanny if I should die, because Kathryn would be burdened with too much responsibility. He reluctantly agreed but didn't want to admit that I *could* die. Kathryn understands the seriousness of cancer, but I doubt that she believes it could take her mother from her. She was not very verbal about the cancer, but it was on her mind. One day, when she met a new neighbor, she matter-of-factly said, "Hi, my mom has cancer." She did express some discontent, however, when she saw me trying on a wig; she didn't like the new look!

My son, Paul, could be described as an average seven year old; he's always asking a million questions. At the breakfast table he often would ask me, "Are you going to get your breasts pumped up today, Mom?" My breasts had become a family project!

Bridget, age five, is a "classic" middle child. She has taught me a lot about patience. Initially, I thought she didn't comprehend the significance of the disease, but one day she said, "Mom, I don't like that word." When I asked her what was the word she didn't like, she replied, "Cancer." Another time she asked me if she would get breast cancer when she grows up. I told her to get breasts before she worried about it!

At two years old, Maureen initially referred to my breasts as "owies." She would often say, "Mama's owies, pump up!" I was with her the day I realized my hair was actually falling out. Although Maureen didn't understand why I was so sad, she did understand sorrow; she put her arms around me to comfort me as I sat and cried.

Children are very perceptive. We couldn't tell them that everything was fine, especially when it didn't seem that way. Flowers and plants were being delivered, meals were coming to the house, conversations were overheard, and there were visits from relatives. We were very open and honest with the children, but honest in an upbeat way, knowing that children have a tendency to react to our reactions!

The cancer diagnosis was a dilemma. The children know that their grandmother died of cancer when I was young. I wanted them to know that my cancer was different and that their mom would be cured. Yet I couldn't exactly guarantee that I would survive their childhood years. When Aunt Kathryn died, I told them she died from breast cancer. I guess I wanted them to be aware of the possibility for me, too. At our dinner table every night, after saying Grace, Kevin and the children added, "And thank you, God, for healing Mom." This gave them reassurance.

I showed the children my mastectomy incisions and the JP tubes when I arrived home from the hospital; I felt it was necessary for them to see what had happened to their mother. It was not difficult for me to do this. I treated it as something that was necessary to remove the cancer. Occasionally the children would come with me to the plastic surgeon and watch as he injected fluid into the implants. They also accompanied me to chemotherapy, observing my blood being drawn and the chemotherapy being administered. I felt that my attitude and acceptance would help them deal with it better.

It haunts me that my life has been threatened and that I could die and leave these wonderful children. Milestones in my life when I missed not having a mother the most were: proms, high school graduation, and college graduation. I planned my own wedding. When our first child was born, how I wished my mother could have seen her. After childbirth, I thought to myself, Now you've made it; you've survived it all without a mother. It wasn't until I was diagnosed with cancer that my need of her flashed back to me. No one can replace a mother's love and comfort and that knowledge haunts me.

I don't know what the future holds for me, but I know that a person my age without the diagnosis of breast cancer statistically has a better chance of being alive ten years from now. I refuse to say I *have* cancer; I say I *had* cancer. Someday I will die, but I know there is a God and a new life waiting for me.

Dear Kathryn, Bridget, and Maureen, I regret having given you the risk of carrying the cancer gene, but maybe I can pass along to you things that are much stronger. Hopefully I can give you a belief in God, my love, a sense of humor, courage, and strength. With these, you too will be survivors. I love you. Paul, I love you too.